MEDICARE FOR YOU

MEDICARE FOR YOU

A Smart Person's Guide

DIANE J. OMDAHL, RN, MS

Humanix Books
www.humanixbooks.com

Humanix Books

MEDICARE FOR YOU
Copyright © 2023 by Diane J. Omdahl
All rights reserved

Humanix Books, P.O. Box 20989, West Palm Beach, FL 33416, USA
www.humanixbooks.com | info@humanixbooks.com

Disclaimer: The information presented in this book is meant to be used for general resource purposes only; it is not intended as specific financial advice for any individual and should not substitute financial advice from a finance professional. Appropriate decisions and actions depend on the exact circumstances, supporting facts, and regional interpretations, so the advice and strategies in this book may not be appropriate for individual situations. Please contact Social Security, Medicare, the specific insurance plan issuers, or other appropriate individuals or agencies for further guidance.

The publisher and the author disclaim any responsibility for positions or actions taken by individuals in reliance on the contents herein and shall not be liable for any damages.

The author does not sell insurance, nor does she work with or for any company that does sell insurance.

ISBN: 9-781-63006-181-4 (Paperback)
ISBN: 9-781-63006-182-1 (E-book)

Printed in the United States of America
10 9 8 7 6 5 4 3 2 1

In memory of Rich, my husband

Contents

Introduction

Just about every day I hear, "How does the normal person do Medicare?" That implies two things. One, people recognize that Medicare is complicated, overwhelming, and confusing. And two, I am not normal.

Yes, I understand Medicare. My business partner, who also happens to be my daughter, often introduces me by saying, "Medicare makes sense to Diane, and that's all you need to know about her."

The subtitle of this book is A Smart Person's Guide. But the smart person I'm referring to isn't me, it's you. By picking up this book, you've proven you're wise enough to know that Medicare needs to make as much sense to you as it does to me. Hopefully, once you've finished reading this book, it will!

Even though I have made every effort to simplify the process, Medicare is a difficult subject. It will take time to work your way through the steps. As you begin your study, know these important points.

- The guidance comes from the Centers for Medicare and Medicaid Services, Social Security, Medicare.gov, and other creditable sources.
- The examples are real. I couldn't make up most of these.
- The selected topics are based on the struggles I have witnessed as people navigate the road to Medicare.

- Content is organized in sequence of "first things first"—get ready, determine your timing, research coverage options, enroll, and live with Medicare.
- In some situations, you may need to do more research or seek qualified help.
- Medicare costs and rules can change. To make sure that you have access to the most current information, bookmark www.dianeomdahl.com/updates.

Chapter 1

Get Ready for Medicare

I have a friend who started training for a 5K marathon. Before she took her first step, she did all kinds of research about physical training, psychological readiness, finances, attire, nutritional regimen, and more. She knew it was important to be prepared and know what she was doing.

Medicare is your marathon.

My friend's journey was 26.2 miles. You are getting ready to start Medicare, a lifelong journey. You should be at least as diligent as a marathoner. This book will guide you as you prepare for and begin your trip.

Basic Terms and Concepts

On your Medicare journey, you'll hear about some unfamiliar terms—Part A, Part B, Medicare Advantage, Medigap policy, Part D drug coverage, and out-of-pocket maximum—that can be confusing and intimidating. They are crucial to your correct interpretation of Medicare information and advertisements. That's why this book starts with an introduction to these terms. You'll learn more important details in the upcoming chapters.

Original Medicare
Also called Traditional Medicare, this refers to just Part A, hospital insurance, and Part B, medical insurance.

Beneficiary
This is an individual enrolled in Medicare.

The Parts of Medicare

We've all heard that Medicare has four parts, and you may be prepared to get all four. However, Medicare really has three essential parts of coverage that work together to meet your medical and medication needs going forward.

- Part A, hospital insurance, covers inpatient stays in a hospital or skilled nursing facility (Medicare-certified nursing home), home health care, and hospice.
- Part B, medical insurance, is the outpatient component of Medicare, which includes doctors' visits, diagnostic tests, and outpatient procedures. Part B also covers many preventive services.
- Part D, prescription drug coverage, is sponsored by private insurance companies and helps cover medications prescribed by a doctor.

The three parts then combine to make the Original Medicare Path and the Medicare Advantage Path.

Original Medicare Path

This path starts with Part A and Part B. For more comprehensive coverage, a beneficiary can add a Medigap policy and Part D drug plan.

Medicare Supplement Insurance or Medigap Policy

Private insurance companies sponsor this health insurance policy that is an important component of the Original Medicare Path. It's commonly called a Medigap policy because it helps cover the gaps in Part A and Part B coverage. The terms "Medicare supplement" and "Medigap policy" can be used interchangeably.

Medicare Advantage Path

Also known as Part C, this is Medicare administered by private insurance companies. A plan can provide Part A, Part B, and

Part D services and additional benefits for one premium. That makes it an alternative to, not a part of, Original Medicare.

Member or Enrollee
This is someone who has purchased an additional plan, such as a Medicare Advantage plan or a Part D drug plan.

Centers for Medicare and Medicaid Services (CMS)
This is the federal agency that administers the Medicare program. It's part of the Department of Health and Human Services.

The Social Security Administration (SSA)
The SSA is the federal agency that administers Social Security, a social insurance program consisting of retirement, disability, and survivor benefits, including Medicare. The SSA is in charge of Medicare enrollment and premiums. The phone number for Social Security is (800) 772-1213, and the website is www.ssa.gov. Local offices have their own phone numbers.

Cost Sharing
There are some who think Medicare is free. However, very few things in life are, and Medicare is definitely not one of those. Cost sharing means you share the costs with Medicare and the applicable insurance companies. Here are cost sharing terms you'll see mentioned many times throughout this book.

- *Premium:* The amount you pay for the coverage every month. Beneficiaries can pay premiums for Part A, Part B, Medicare Advantage and Part D drug plans, and Medigap policies. Higher-income beneficiaries pay additional amounts.
- *Deductible:* The amount you pay for covered health care services before the coverage starts to pay. Part A, Part B, Medigap policies, and Medicare Advantage and Part D drug plans can all have deductibles.
- *Copayment:* A fixed amount, like $20, you pay for each service after meeting the deductible.

- *Coinsurance:* A percentage of costs, such as 20 percent, you pay after meeting the deductible.
- *Out-of-pocket limit or maximum:* The most you will pay for covered services in a plan year. Medicare Advantage plans and some Medigap policies have these limits.

This book incorporates 2022 costs. Every November, Medicare releases premiums and costs for the next year. Check www.dianeomdahl.com/updates for updated information.

Guaranteed Issue Right

The Affordable Care Act (ACA) eliminated the impact of pre-existing medical conditions on some insurance applications. Companies cannot deny coverage because of any health problems one has before applying for a policy.

However, the ACA does not apply to Medicare. Preexisting medical conditions can have an impact on your ability to get a Medigap policy. If you have a guaranteed issue right, you can purchase a Medigap policy without going through medical underwriting. The insurance company cannot deny the application or charge higher premiums because of pre-existing conditions. You'll learn more about this in upcoming chapters. But for now, if you know about timing, you'll be able to get the coverage you want.

Tips to Help You Get Ready

Once you enter the Medicare arena, you'll have your hands full with enrollment, choosing coverage, and figuring it all out. Here are eight tips to help you get ready so you aren't overwhelmed.

1. Buy a bigger mailbox, get another recycling bin, and put new batteries in your remote control.

This is a tongue-in-cheek way of preparing you for the onslaught of Medicare advertisements and mailings you'll face as you approach age 65. You're going to get so much mail from so many companies about so many plans that you may need another mailbox so there is room for your bills. Don't try to digest all that; instead, recycle it.

If you watch TV, you'll likely see a steady stream of Medicare commercials, narrated by football MVPs, television celebrities, and "everyday" people. To keep from getting overwhelmed, hit the mute button on your remote. Backup batteries will guarantee a little peace during dinner.

2. Establish or update your financial and medical powers of attorney.

A power of attorney (POA) is a powerful thing. A financial POA document allows an appointed person to make financial, legal, and property decisions on another individual's behalf. A person holding another's POA can sell the individual's car to pay medical bills, for example. A medical POA is a durable POA for health care. This allows an agent (a trusted friend or family member) to make important and necessary health care decisions if the individual becomes incapacitated or unable to communicate or participate in care. With this authority, the POA can make health care decisions for a patient on a ventilator or in a coma. Establishing powers of attorney must be done while a person is of sound mind and able to make financial and medical decisions.

If you have executed your POAs, great. Review the documents to make sure they are current and reflect your wishes.

If you have no POAs, do that now. You never know what might happen tomorrow. There are so many decisions to make.

- What powers do you want to give to your agent?
- Do you want more than one person to serve as your agent?
- Will the document address long-term care (LTC) costs?
- What state laws govern the execution of the agreement?

There are online forms available, so you could save on the attorney's fees. However, given that these documents will dictate your future health and financial decisions, consider getting legal advice from an estate-planning attorney.

Jumping ahead: You'll learn in chapter 8, "Medicare and Social Security Representatives," that POAs are not enough for Medicare or Social Security. Once enrolled, be sure to take care of what's necessary.

3. Confirm your eligibility for Medicare.

There are two components to eligibility.

1. *Are you eligible to enroll in Medicare?*
   You will be able to enroll in Medicare if you are age 65 or older and a citizen or legal permanent resident of the United States for at least five years. Younger people with disabilities, end-stage renal disease (ESRD or permanent kidney failure requiring dialysis or transplant), or amyotrophic lateral sclerosis (or Lou Gehrig's disease) can also qualify when meeting the requirements.
2. *Are you eligible for premium-free Part A, hospital insurance?*
   If you are eligible for Medicare, then you must determine whether you qualify for premium-free Part A. If so, you would not have to pay the monthly premium.
   Most are eligible if they or their spouse worked and paid Medicare taxes for at least 10 years and have earned 40 Social Security credits. (See chap. 1, "Questions and Answers about Getting Ready for Medicare.")
   Those who have not worked enough quarters and do not qualify for premium-free Part A can purchase it. (See chap. 7, "Premiums for Medicare Coverage.")

Confirm your eligibility at www.medicare-links.com/my-ssa-account.

A Domestic Partner

The eligibility requirements state that a person can qualify for premium-free Medicare based on a spouse's employment history. There is no mention of qualifying through a domestic partner. Partners may be eligible to get insurance through the partner's employment. However, things change when Medicare enters the picture because they are not married to each other. A person cannot qualify for Medicare based on a partner's employment. (See chap. 3, "Know When You Need More Help.")

---

4. Establish a *my* Social Security account.

Have you given any thought to how you plan to enroll in Medicare? Years ago, it was common to hop in the car and visit the local Social Security office. Then Social Security started offering in-person and phone appointments. With the onslaught of Boomers turning 65, Social Security has encouraged online enrollment, which basically became the only way to enroll during the COVID pandemic when the offices were closed.

According to Social Security, enrolling online can take less than 10 minutes with no forms to sign and usually no documentation to submit. Online enrollment sounds like a great way to enroll, but there's one catch. You need a *my* Social Security account to do this.

If you already have an account, take a few minutes to log in now (whether you're 45, 65, or anywhere in between). Make sure you can access it successfully so you'll be ready when it's time. Social Security has procedures for retrieving or changing your username and password if necessary.

If you don't have an account, establish one now. During the process, Social Security will verify your identity against their records. In the case of discrepancies, the system will lock out the user. Those issues can take time to resolve.

If you have problems establishing or accessing your account, contact Social Security at (800) 772-1213.

5. Remember to record all relevant interactions and save important documents.

I have talked with many individuals who were late enrolling in Part B, medical insurance, or missed their chance completely. In some cases, they will tell me that a person with Social Security or Medicare told them what to do, and it turned out to be wrong information.

If an individual in a position of authority, such as a Social Security agent, provides wrong information, the misdirected individual may have a basis for getting the situation corrected. To do that, there must be proof of error, misrepresentation, or inaction by a federal employee. The proof starts with the details of the initial interaction, including the date, time, name of the employee, and complete details. Without that, there is little chance to prove a case. And in most of the conversations I had, the individuals had no recollection of who they spoke with or when they received the misinformation.

It's also a good idea to keep any relevant information, such as the Annual Notice of Changes, creditable prescription drug notices, and any application or appeal submitted.

6. Do your homework and determine what's best for you.

Just about everyone has had coverage through an employer group health plan. The plan's package of benefits and costs applies to anyone who has the coverage, without consideration of an individual's unique situation or needs. Spouses can have the same coverage as the employee.

That changes in the Medicare world. Medicare is a one-person, one-plan deal. Your Medicare plan cannot cover your spouse or children. You need to find coverage that will work for you, not only when you are spry and healthy at age 65, but down the road, as you age and face health challenges. This probably won't be the same coverage your spouse or best friend has.

7. Consider enlisting the services of a financial advisor or an accountant.

As you read this book, you'll quickly discover how costs and financial considerations have a big impact on Medicare decisions. What do you do with a Health Savings Account (HSA)? Are you a higher-income beneficiary? How will you handle out-of-pocket costs? Can you afford LTC?

Getting help from a professional will keep you on the right track.

8. Know when to take action.

When it comes to tackling Medicare, there seem to be two responses. People get nervous and rush ahead blindly. They may do exactly what a friend did without even checking out how that would work for them. Or they procrastinate and drag their feet. It never fails; they become frantic as deadlines approach, and then they run into problems.

To help your Medicare journey go as smoothly as possible, figure out the right time to take action, and then develop a plan.

Questions and Answers about Getting Ready for Medicare

Why do some people get incorrect advice from Social Security?

You probably think that Social Security agents should know the answers to any question they get. However, consider this: Social Security has over 2,700 rules but just one phone number. When you call that number, there is no "push 1 for retirement benefits," "push 2 for disability benefits," and so on. Instead, no matter your issue, the next available agent will answer the call. If you have an issue that is not ordinary, the agent may not know all the details about that. Sometimes the best advice is to hang up and call again.

How do I set up a *my* Social Security account?

Here are the instructions for establishing an account.

1. You must be at least 18 years old, have a Social Security number, and have a valid U.S. mailing address and email address.
2. Visit www.medicare-links.com/my-ssa-account and select "create an account."
3. Agree to the terms of service and verify your identity.
4. Create your account detail.
5. Enter the security code you receive.

Must I have a *my* Social Security account?

If you are not planning to enroll in Medicare anytime soon or are already enrolled, you can probably do without an account. However, the account will certainly streamline your Medicare application, if you are not yet enrolled. You'll also be able to access all kinds of information about your Social Security benefits, update your address, and more.

How do I get premium-free Part A on my spouse's employment record?

In any situation, your spouse must have paid Medicare taxes for 10 years (earned 40 credits) and be eligible for Social Security benefits (age 62 or older). Then the rules vary slightly.

- You can qualify on your current spouse's employment record if you have been married for at least a year.
- If you are divorced, you will be eligible if that marriage lasted at least 10 years and you are now single.
- To qualify on the record of your spouse who died, you had to be married for at least nine months and currently single.

Can I qualify for Medicare if I am 52 years old with serious health problems?

The original Medicare legislation, passed into law in 1965, provided coverage for those 65 years and older. Over time, eligibility has expanded to include those under age 65 with certain disabilities and medical conditions.

Just because you have health issues doesn't mean you'll qualify for Medicare. The criteria for getting Medicare under age 65 are very specific. It's possible you may have to wait until age 65 to get Medicare.

If I applied for Social Security retirement benefits six months ago at age 62, why haven't I received my Medicare card?

You likely have heard that those who are receiving Social Security retirement benefits are enrolled automatically in Medicare. However, you must also be eligible for Medicare, which means you're 65 years or older.

Can I apply for Medicaid at the same time I apply for Medicare?

Medicare and Medicaid are two separate federal health insurance programs.

- Medicare is for people age 65 or older and certain younger people with disabilities or ESRD.
- Medicaid is a program for eligible low-income and elderly adults, children, pregnant women, and those with

disabilities, funded jointly by states and the federal government. States administer the program, so every state has its own criteria and processes.

Visit www.medicare-links.com/apply-for-medicaid to learn more and see whether you qualify and how to get started.

These tips are an introduction to important things you need to know and do. And with that, we'll segue into the next chapter. You'll learn about different enrollment situations and figure out exactly when you need to take your first steps.

Chapter 2

Determine Your Timing

Boomers may remember a song from the early '60s by Jimmy Jones about how we need timing, good timing, timing is the thing. But in too many cases, figuring out Medicare timing (i.e., when you need to enroll) is important and frequently overlooked. So many Medicare resources skip right over this timing step and jump into talking about plans you need. You could end up enrolling when you don't need to or not enrolling when you must, mistakes that can carry considerable costs in dollars. Some of the most expensive mistakes I have seen can also jeopardize coverage, possibly for years.

This chapter will help you evaluate your current situation, determine your timing, and figure out your first steps.

Medicare has dozens of enrollment periods. These give people the chance to get additional coverage, address changes in personal circumstances, even right past wrongs. In this book, you'll read about several.

However, there are three important ones that deal with enrolling in Medicare.

- *Initial Enrollment Period (IEP):* The time for everyone turning 65 to pay attention.
- *Part B Special Enrollment Period (SEP):* An opportunity for those who retire after age 65.
- *General Enrollment Period (GEP):* Oops, you missed your chance.

Turning 65: The Initial Enrollment Period (IEP)

Must You Enroll in Medicare at Age 65?

The answer is no. There is no requirement you must enroll in Medicare at age 65. But many, many approaching their 65th birthday have read or been told that, *no matter their situation, they must enroll in Medicare.*

I have been caught in arguments with those who enrolled in Medicare because they "had to" but now realize they made a mistake by enrolling when it wasn't necessary.

You'll learn that some are enrolled automatically, several will need to enroll, and others can delay enrollment. You must evaluate your situation and determine whether or not you should enroll in Medicare.

What to Know about the IEP

The IEP is probably the most important Medicare enrollment period. This is the chance for those turning 65 to determine what they must do *right now*. It applies to every single individual who is eligible for Medicare, no matter their circumstances—whether they're married, working, retired, or whatever else.

Know these important facts.

- The IEP is a seven-month period that begins three months before and ends three months after the month of your 65th birthday.
- If you enroll during the first three months, Medicare will begin on the first day of your birth month.

  > Dana's birthday is April 15. His IEP begins January 1 and ends July 31. If he enrolls during the first three months of the IEP, Part A and Part B will take effect on April 1.

- However, for those born on the first day of a month, the IEP shifts one month earlier.

  > Dana's girlfriend was born on April Fools' Day. Her IEP begins December 1 and will end June 30. If she enrolls during the first three months, Part A and Part B will begin on March 1.

- You can enroll during the last four months of the IEP. If enrolling in 2023 or beyond, Part A will take effect as in the examples above and Part B will start the first day of the month after you enroll.

(If you are turning 65 in 2022, see www.dianeomdahl .com/updates for more about your IEP.)

As you approach your 65th birthday, evaluate your circumstances and determine what you should or shouldn't do.

How to Navigate This Chapter

- Look over all the informational headings.
- Keep in mind the specifics of your situation: age, employment, health status, retirement goals, and anything else that could affect the timing of your Medicare enrollment.
- Choose your situation and follow the guidance.

Identify Your Situation

Those turning 65 may be working and have employer coverage, or they may already be retired. It's possible they have a Marketplace plan they want to replace. You'll find your situation in this chapter, identifying the decisions you should make and the actions you need to take.

You Don't Have 40 Social Security Credits

Important: The following situations and the related instructions apply to those who qualify for premium-free Part A, hospital insurance. They or a spouse have paid Medicare taxes for at least 10 years (40 quarters) and earned 40 credits.

But what if you don't have 40 credits?

Decision: How and when will you enroll?
  If you don't have 40 credits, your enrollment instructions may be very different.
Actions: According to the Centers for Medicare and Medicaid Services (CMS), you must do the following
  - file an enrollment application by contacting Social Security,
  - enroll during your IEP, and

- enroll in Part B, medical insurance, mandatory for those who do not have 40 credits.

Now if you do qualify for premium-free Part A, find your situation, make your decisions, and then act.

You Are Receiving Social Security Retirement Benefits Prior to Age 65

Years ago, a federal lawsuit determined that Medicare is a condition of receiving benefits. So everyone who receives retirement benefits will be enrolled automatically in Medicare Part A and Part B, and their Medicare card will arrive in the mail. They must keep Part A, at a minimum, or else they forfeit their retirement benefits.

Decision: Should you keep Part B?
  The type of insurance you have at age 65 drives your decision as to whether Part B is necessary.
Actions:
  - Find your existing coverage in the following list and learn what to do about Part B.
  - If you must keep it, verify the accuracy of the information on your Medicare card and keep it safe.
  - If you determine that Part B is not necessary, you must decline it before the effective date. The instructions with the Medicare card explain what to do. (See chap. 2, "Questions and Answers about the IEP.")
    Note: For residents of Puerto Rico who receive Social Security benefits, the situation is reversed. They will get Medicare Part A automatically at age 65, but if they need Part B, they must enroll by completing one form, the Application for Enrollment in Part B. (See chap. 4, "Enrolling in Medicare.")

You Are Still Working with Coverage through an Employer Group Health Plan (EGHP)

Here's another top 10 question for those approaching age 65.

"Must I apply for Medicare if I am still working?"

Too many times, those who ask this get a quick answer, like you don't have to enroll if you keep working, or you have to enroll in Medicare even if you're working. Either answer can be right or wrong depending on the individual circumstances.

The Medicare decision hinges on the number of employees in the company sponsoring the group plan. This is the actual number of employees, not the number covered by the group plan. For Medicare purposes, companies are divided into those with 20 or more employees and companies with fewer than 20 employees.

1. *EGHP sponsored by a company with 20 or more employees (referred to in this book as a large employer).*
   By law, this employer plan cannot change the rules for either the employee or dependents (Medicare-eligible spouses). The company cannot drop the coverage, charge more, or make anyone enroll in Medicare. It's as though the 65th birthday never happens.
   Decision: What do you want to do about your plan and Medicare?
   It's up to you. You can continue with the group plan, or you can drop the coverage and enroll in Medicare. (See chap. 2, "Questions and Answers about the IEP.")
   Actions: If you decide to continue with the EGHP, know that enrolling in Part B if you have a large employer plan could jeopardize your future Medicare options. (See chap. 3, "Questions and Answers about Changing Paths.") Then choose the appropriate action.
   - If you are receiving Social Security retirement benefits, decline Part B. Follow the instructions to return the Medicare card.

- If you plan to apply for Social Security retirement benefits, enroll in Part A.
- If you plan to delay retirement benefits, evaluate the benefits of enrolling in Part A. This can be a plus. (See chap. 2, "Questions and Answers about the IEP.")
- If you have a high-deductible health plan and want to continue contributions to a Health Savings Account (HSA), do not enroll in Part A or Social Security. (See chap. 2, "Keeping Employer Group Coverage Past Age 65.")

2. *EGHP sponsored by a company with fewer than 20 employees (referred to in this book as a small employer).* The rules change when someone has coverage through a small employer. It is up to the company whether you can continue with the group plan after age 65.

- If you can, Medicare laws dictate that this employer plan will be the secondary payer (Medicare is first), so you must enroll in Medicare. (See chap. 2, "Questions and Answers about the IEP.")
- If you cannot keep this coverage, you must enroll in Medicare and then choose your Medicare path. (See chap. 3, "The Two Medicare Paths.")

Decision: There is no decision to make about Medicare. Whether you can or can't keep the small employer plan, you must enroll in Part A, hospital insurance, and Part B, medical insurance. If you can keep the plan, decide whether you will.

Actions:

- Enroll in Part A and Part B during your IEP.
- If keeping the plan, get documentation that you can, such as a copy of the company policy.
- If contributing to an HSA, stop contributions before Medicare takes effect.

You Are a Spouse with Coverage through an EGHP Owned by Your Spouse Who Is Still Working

Decision: What do you want to do about your plan and Medicare?

Just as with your working spouse, the number of employees in the company drives your actions.

Actions:

- Determine whether your coverage is sponsored by a large or small employer.
- Check out that section, then get to work.

You Do Not Have Coverage Now, or You Will Give Up Existing Coverage at Age 65

There are some plans that will disappear at age 65, leaving an individual without coverage. Many choose to retire and have no options for coverage in retirement. Others may not have medical insurance, for whatever reason. In these situations, enrollment in Part A and Part B is necessary.

Decision: There is no decision since you must enroll in Medicare.

Actions:

- Identify your IEP and enroll in Medicare Part A and Part B, preferably during the first month. This will give Social Security plenty of time to process your application.
- Choose your Medicare path. (See chap. 3, "The Two Medicare Paths.")

You Have COBRA, Retiree, Individual, or Veteran Affairs Coverage

By law, these types of coverage become secondary to Medicare after age 65. That means they work with Medicare to pay your claims to the allowable limits. Without Medicare, a secondary payer won't pay anything. (See chap. 2, "Questions and Answers about the IEP.")

Decision: Determine whether you can and want to continue with this coverage at age 65.

In most cases, those who accept Consolidated Omnibus Budget Reconciliation Act (COBRA) coverage before age 65 will discover it ends as of their 65th birthday. Many retiree plans offer coverage after age 65. It may be possible to keep an individual plan; however, the costs may be prohibitive, and Medicare offers a better option.

Actions:

- Enroll in Medicare Part A and Part B during your IEP.
- If you can and want to keep this coverage, chapter 3, "Know When You Need More Help," addresses important points.
- If you cannot or do not want to keep this coverage, choose your Medicare path. (See chap. 3, "The Two Medicare Paths.")

You Have a Federal Employee Health Benefits (FEHB) Plan, Whether Working, Retired, or a Spouse

This coverage will continue to be the primary payer after age 65. The plan cannot force anyone to enroll in Medicare.

Decisions:

- Will you enroll in Medicare Part A?
  If you plan to apply for Social Security retirement benefits, Part A enrollment is a must and could provide some benefits. (See chap. 2, "Questions and Answers about the IEP.")
- Will you enroll in Part B?
  This is a completely different situation for FEHB plan members because there is no mandate;

however, there can be repercussions if they're not enrolled. (See chap. 3, "Know When You Need More Help.")

Actions:

- If you are still working as a federal employee with an HSA, delay Medicare enrollment. (See chap. 2, "Keeping Employer Group Coverage Past Age 65.")
- If applying for Social Security retirement benefits, enroll in Part A, then decide what to do about Medicare Part B.
- If not contributing to an HSA or you are retired or the spouse of an FEHB policy owner, consider enrollment in Part A and evaluate the Part B situation.

Keeping Employer Group Coverage Past Age 65

If you're thinking about working past age 65 and keeping your employer coverage, you aren't alone. According to a recent American Advisors Group survey, almost one-fifth (18 percent) of respondents said they will work past the age of 70. Besides figuring out what to do when you finally decide to retire, there are three important issues that you can't ignore before then. (These issues can also apply if you have an EGHP through your spouse.)

1. Creditable prescription drug coverage.

Because your employer plan probably includes drug coverage, you likely will not enroll in a Medicare Part D drug plan. That makes sense. Why pay for duplicative coverage? However, the coverage must be creditable and meet Medicare's criteria (yes, there are criteria for this too) or you will face penalties when enrolling in a Part D plan later.

Creditable drug coverage, in simple terms, means it pays at least as much as the standard Medicare drug plan. If your employer's drug coverage is creditable, you do not need to purchase a Part D prescription drug plan as long as you keep that plan. When you decide to give up this coverage or it ends, you will have a chance to purchase a Part D plan without facing a late enrollment penalty.

Companies that provide drug coverage must notify those over 65 as to whether or not the coverage is creditable. (This is not the same notice you get every year about creditable medical coverage.) During your IEP, it's a good idea to ask a plan administrator for a copy of the current creditable drug notice. Then, after you turn 65, pay attention to notices from the plan's sponsor. By law, the sponsor must send a notice by October 15 every year.

I have asked many who kept the group plan whether they received a notice. Most say, "I don't think so." But the honest ones remember getting something about the plan's drug coverage, but it didn't make sense. Look for the words, "Your existing coverage is considered creditable," which is good; you don't need to enroll in a drug plan or worry about penalties. Save the notices you get every year, just in case there are questions from the drug plan when you decide to get Part D coverage.

If the EGHP does not have creditable drug coverage, consider enrolling in a Part D prescription drug plan during your IEP. You would need to enroll in Medicare Part A first to qualify for drug coverage. If you delay, you will face a Part D late enrollment penalty for every month you go without creditable coverage.

> Samuel has been covered under his wife's employer group health plan since he was 60 years old. She decided to retire at age 65, when he was 73. Then he discovered the drug coverage he had for all those years was not considered creditable. He paid a late enrollment penalty of $32 a month in 2022. That amount will change, and he'll pay the penalty

for the rest of his life. (See chap. 2, "Questions and Answers about the IEP.")

2. Health Savings Account (HSA).

An HSA raises many questions and can cause problems if you don't understand the rules.

If you are contributing to an HSA and enroll in Medicare, either just Part A or Part A and Part B, you must stop contributions. Those enrolled in Medicare are no longer eligible to contribute to an HSA. Contributions made after enrolling are not deductible and subject to an excise tax.

If you continue working, the size of the company determines whether you must stop contributions.

- If the company has fewer than 20 employees, you must enroll in Medicare Part A and Part B to have complete coverage. You should stop contributions at age 65.
- If the company has 20 or more employees, you can defer Medicare enrollment and continue contributions. However, if you enroll after age 65, Social Security can backdate the effective date for Part A up to six months. You should stop contributions six months before you want Medicare to take effect, so you don't run into any problems.
- Also know that you would need to prorate contributions. For example, if Medicare takes effect June 1, you can contribute 5/12 or one-half of the annual allowance.

What if you don't know about the rules and continue contributions when you shouldn't? There are some actions you can take to undo the contributions, depending on the specifics and timing of your situation. Because this gets complicated, consider consulting with a tax advisor.

After retirement, you can withdraw funds from the HSA for eligible medical expenses, including premiums for Medicare Part B, medical insurance, and Part D, prescription drug coverage, and a Medicare Advantage plan, along with deductibles, copayments, and coinsurance for medical care and medications. Financial advisors suggest you consider saving the HSA to help with long-term care expenses.

One caveat: You cannot use funds from an HSA to pay premiums for a Medigap policy.

If you are the spouse, your decision to enroll in Medicare does not have an impact on the working spouse's ability to contribute to an HSA. Funds from the HSA can pay for your qualified medical expenses.

An HSA can be complicated and confusing. Consult with a trusted financial advisor or accountant to determine what is best in your situation.

3. Changing jobs after age 65.

In the next chapter, you'll learn about the Part B Special Enrollment Period (SEP) if you work past age 65. When ready to retire, you can determine when you need Medicare to start and you won't face any late enrollment penalties. However, you will need to prove to Social Security that you qualify for the SEP. (This also applies to the spouse if the employee changes jobs.)

There are two important Part B SEP criteria.

- At age 65, you have coverage through an EGHP related to the current employment of you or your spouse.
- Between age 65 and your retirement date, there are no lapses of eight months or longer in employment or coverage.

There is one form—Request for Employment Information (CMS-L564)—that will prove you meet the criteria. (Learn more about this form in chapter 4, "Over 65: Enrolling in Medicare.")

If you have just one job from age 65 until retirement, you need only one form to support your Medicare application. However, if you have more than one job, you will need forms from every employer to prove you meet the criteria.

> Gloria had five sales jobs between age 65 and 72, when she retired. A couple of the companies were no longer in business. She had a very difficult time proving she was employed and had coverage for those seven years.

To avoid trying to get documentation from past employers to support your application for Medicare at retirement, consider this. Before walking out the door of any job you leave after age 65, get the Request for Employment Information form completed. Then, if you plan to get another job, do it as soon as possible to avoid any eight-month gaps.

Questions and Answers about the IEP

Why would I decline or not enroll in Part B if I am still working for a company with 20 or more employees?

If you have coverage through this company, Part B enrollment is not a good idea for three reasons.

1. You will incur additional costs. Part B is optional because you would have to pay the Part B premium every month. Because you are still earning a salary, it's possible that you could be considered a higher-income beneficiary and have to pay more. (See chap. 7, "IRMAA.")
2. Part B coverage may not add any benefits to the group plan. If so, you would be spending money for no reason.

3. The most important reason is that, depending on where you live, you could jeopardize your future Medicare options and not be able to get the coverage you want. (See chap. 3, "Questions and Answers about Changing Paths down the Road.")

As long as you (or your spouse) continue to work with coverage sponsored by a large employer, you will have a special opportunity to enroll in Part B. (See chap. 2, "Over 65: The Part B Special Enrollment Period [SEP].")

If I have coverage through a small employer plan and have to enroll in Medicare, wouldn't that jeopardize my future Medicare options, just as discussed in the previous question?

Unlike those who have coverage sponsored by a large employer, you must enroll in Medicare in order to have complete coverage. By law, a small employer plan is the secondary payer to Medicare.

Because you are "forced" to enroll in Medicare, different rules apply. If you know what to do, you won't jeopardize your options. You will have time to get the coverage you want. (See chap. 3, "Changing Paths down the Road.")

How do I decline Part B?

If you're receiving Social Security retirement benefits and are enrolled in Medicare automatically, you will receive your Medicare card in the mail. It is a perforated cutout in the middle of a set of instructions. If you decide that you don't need Part B, you have to return the card to Social Security. Do not punch out the card; return the entire page by the effective date to the address noted.

If you punch out the card and throw away the instructions, you may have to call Social Security to figure out what to do.

If I don't have to enroll in Medicare, why should I consider Part A?

If you are not contributing to an HSA, there are some good reasons you might want Part A.

- This is premium-free coverage for those who qualify through their work history or that of a spouse.
- Part A can help cover the costs for hospitalization, skilled nursing facility stays, home health care, or hospice. (See chap. 3, "The Three Parts of Medicare and Costs Overview.")
- You could also have a greater choice of providers and facilities.

Caution: If there might be a future opportunity for you to contribute to an HSA, think carefully about your Part A decision. According to CMS, because this is a free benefit, it is illegal to disenroll or drop Part A once you've got it.

What is the Part B late enrollment penalty?

This penalty applies to those who do not enroll in Part B when they should. They missed their IEP and don't qualify for a Part B SEP, or they qualified for an SEP but didn't enroll before it ended.

There are two parts to the penalty.

1. *Additional premiums:* They will pay 10 percent of the standard Part B premium for every year (a full 12 months) they delayed enrollment. In 2022, the penalty amount was $17.10 (10 percent of $170.10). Three years late enrolling in Part B added $51.30 to the monthly premium.
2. *Delayed coverage:* They cannot enroll in Part B until the GEP, January 1–March 31.

How can I avoid the penalty?

Know when you must enroll (during either your IEP or Part B SEP) and do it on time.

Can you explain the Part D late enrollment penalty?

Those over the age of 65 who do not have creditable prescription drug coverage for two or more months will pay 1 percent of the current standard Part D premium for every month without creditable drug coverage.

In 2022, the penalty amount was $0.33 (1 percent of $33). Not having creditable drug coverage for 106 months added $35 to the monthly premium bill.

If not enrolling in a Part D drug plan at age 65, verify the status of your drug coverage. If it is not creditable, consider enrolling in a drug plan or pay the penalty.

Medicare's Late Enrollment Penalties

Jump offsides and that's a penalty in football. Pay your taxes late and you face an IRS penalty. And if you miss something when getting into Medicare, there are penalties for not enrolling when you should.

Know the penalty amounts for Part A, Part B, and Part D can change every year. Plus, the penalties for Part B and Part D are lifelong; they do not go away.

Are there any red flags that an employer's plan may not have creditable prescription drug coverage?

Probably the biggest red flag is a high-deductible plan. If the plan does not cover medications until the deductible is met, that drug coverage is likely not creditable. The reason why is the plan's deductible cannot be more than the one Medicare sets for Part D drug plans.

If Part A is premium-free, why is there a late enrollment penalty?

The penalty applies to those who have not earned 40 retirement credits. They must enroll in Part A during their IEP. If they don't, they will pay 10 percent of the Part A premium in effect for the calendar year for twice as many years as they were late enrolling.

A beneficiary three years late enrolling in Part A would pay a penalty amount every month for six years. The penalty amount in 2022 for those who have 30–39 credits was $27.40 and $49.40 for those with fewer than 30 credits.

If you don't have 40 credits, through either your employment history or that of a spouse, enroll in Part A during your IEP.

What are primary and secondary payers?

Primary and secondary payers come into play when someone has coverage other than Medicare after age 65. The primary payer is the insurer that pays a health care bill first. The secondary payer covers any remaining costs, up to its limits. You need both pieces to get the best coverage.

In many cases, the primary payer drives the Medicare enrollment decision. A group health plan sponsored by a company with 20 or more employees is, by law, the primary payer. That plan pays a medical claim up to its limits. That's why those who have this coverage can defer Medicare enrollment.

Medicare is the primary payer for a beneficiary with coverage other than a large EGHP. If the Medicare-approved amount for an outpatient procedure is $300, Medicare Part B pays 80 percent, which would be $240. The secondary insurance would be responsible for 20 percent, or the remaining $60.

Without Medicare, there are no claims for the secondary payer to pay. It would be like having no insurance at all.

(There is one exception to Medicare being the primary payer, and it applies to those who have coverage through an FEHB plan. Chapter 3, "Know When You Need More Help," addresses this issue.)

How can I determine the number of employees in my company?

The number of employees in the company sponsoring a group health plan is the total number of employees, not just those who have insurance. This is the most important factor in deciding whether you can delay Medicare enrollment at age 65. If you work for a Fortune 500 company or a health system, there is little doubt that there are 20 or more employees.

However, it's more difficult to determine numbers for small businesses, especially given the fluctuations in employment during the COVID pandemic. CMS has developed very specific guidelines for determining employer size. Ask a human resources (HR) representative about the size of the company.

How does a multiemployer group health plan figure into an enrollment decision?

A multiemployer group health plan is one sponsored jointly, or contributed to, by two or more employers or unions. Briefly, it is a way for smaller businesses to offer better benefits because there are more covered individuals in the plan.

For Medicare purposes, generally, if at least one company in the group has 20 or more employees, the group plan would be the primary payer. That's because anyone with that plan is considered to have coverage sponsored by a company with 20 or more employees. If no company in the group has 20 or more, everyone would have a small employer plan (fewer than 20 employees).

Contact the benefits administrator or an HR representative to confirm the status of your employer.

Should I ever give up the employer coverage and enroll in Medicare?

With any employer health plan, you can always decide not to continue with the coverage and choose Medicare. There are some factors to consider.

- Do you have any dependents on the plan? Medicare is a one-person, one-plan deal, so there is no coverage for dependents. Your spouse or children would have to find other coverage if you opt for Medicare.
- Are you OK with the costs in your plan? Consider the popular high-deductible health plan. I once heard an agent say that this coverage was great for the "super healthy and the really sick." The healthy incur very few bills. The sick could hit the deductible in a few months, and then the plan would pay 100 percent of all bills. The average individual could end up paying costs throughout the year and never meet the deductible. Medicare might offer some alternatives. But remember, Medicare premiums factor into the equation.
- Can you choose doctors and other providers? Some group plan networks can be restrictive. Medicare might offer a greater choice.
- How good is the plan's benefit package (dental, vision, other covered items)? Depending on the type of coverage, Medicare might or might not be better.

There is no easy answer to whether you should give up employer coverage. Everyone's situation is unique. It's a good idea to do a cost-benefit analysis. If you determine Medicare is a better option, you can drop this coverage and enroll in Medicare. (See chap. 4, "Enrolling in Medicare.")

If I enroll in Medicare, what can I do about health insurance for my children?

Because Medicare is a one-person, one-plan type of coverage, your children will have to find other coverage.

When you enroll in Medicare, your children will experience an involuntary loss of coverage. No matter when this happens, the loss of coverage is a qualifying event to trigger a special Affordable Care Act (ACA) enrollment opportunity. They will have 60 days to enroll in a Marketplace plan.

If the company sponsoring your health insurance has 20 or more employees, you could also elect COBRA continuation coverage on behalf of your children.

You should consult with an HR representative or investigate Marketplace plans at www.medicare-links.com/marketplace -plans.

If I enroll in Medicare, do I have to stop contributions to a Flexible Spending Arrangement (FSA)?

This account allows you to put pre-tax payroll deductions into a special account that you can use to pay for certain medical and dependent care expenses. Your Medicare decision does not have an impact on an FSA, as it does with an HSA. However, know that you cannot use FSA distributions to pay Medicare premiums.

Could I sue if my small employer drops me from my group plan because I turned 65?

There are many websites that say it is not legal for an employer to remove an employee from group coverage just because that person is 65. These websites base that information on two federal regulations.

- Title 42, The Public Health and Welfare, §1395y: "A group health plan shall provide that any individual age 65 or older (and the spouse age 65 or older of any individual) who has current employment status with an employer shall be entitled to the same benefits under the plan under the same conditions as any such individual (or spouse) under age 65." Translation: The employer cannot change the coverage rules just because someone turns 65.

- The Age Discrimination in Employment Act of 1967 (ADEA): "It is unlawful to discriminate against a person because of his or her age with respect to any term, condition, or privilege of employment." The ADEA prohibits employers from denying benefits to older employees.

However, you need to know the rest of the rules.

- Title 42 notes that the clause (quoted above) does not apply to "a group health plan unless the plan is a plan of, or contributed to by, an employer that has 20 or more employees for each working day in each of 20 or more calendar weeks in the current calendar year or the preceding calendar year." The requirements only apply to large employers, not those with fewer than 20 employees.
- The ADEA "applies to private employers with 20 or more employees, state and local governments, employment agencies, labor organizations and the federal government." Small employers are not subject to age discrimination requirements.

If you work for a small employer, know that these employers have different rules.

Over 65: The Part B Special Enrollment Period (SEP)

A special enrollment period can occur at any time after the IEP has ended. A qualifying event in a person's life triggers an SEP, which allows that person to take Medicare action. I have dealt with over two dozen of these special periods, such as those caused by moving in and out of an institution, involuntary loss of coverage, and even one involving retroactive entitlement. However, there is one SEP that can apply to anyone who has employer group coverage at age 65. That is the Part B SEP.

Suppose you decide to keep working past age 65 and continue with the EGHP. Or your spouse is still working, and you have coverage through her group plan. You might have enrolled in Part A, hospital insurance, at age 65, or maybe you didn't do anything about Medicare. In either case, you did not enroll in Part B, medical insurance. Now retirement is on the horizon, and you need to figure out what to do.

That's when the Part B SEP comes into play.

As you read in chapter 2, those who have coverage sponsored by a company with 20 or more employees can defer Part B enrollment. It is optional because of the premium, and it's not recommended because it may jeopardize future Medicare options. (See chap. 3, "Questions and Answers about Changing Paths.") When it's time to retire and give up the employer coverage, the Part B SEP provides an opportunity to enroll on your timetable and not face a late enrollment penalty or delay in coverage at retirement.

The Part B SEP allows you to enroll during the following periods.

- At any time while you still have the employer's coverage. To avoid paying premiums unnecessarily, start the process two or three months before you need Part B to begin. This is the preferred timing because it will avoid gaps in coverage.

  Raymond planned to retire November 30, and his coverage would end December 31. He needs Part B as of January 1. He can start the enrollment process October 1, specifying the January start date.

- Within an eight-month period that begins the month after employment or coverage ends, *whichever comes first.*

  During the COVID pandemic, Gary was "downsized" at the end of November. He thought he would be called back, but that didn't happen. He realized in April that he'd better enroll in Medicare. His Part B SEP began December 1 (his last day of employment was November 30) and will end July 31. Part B will take effect on the first of the month after he enrolls.

You must meet two important criteria to qualify for a Part B SEP.

1. At age 65, you must have coverage through an EGHP that is connected to either your current job or that of your spouse.
2. Until you decide to enroll in Part B, there can be no gaps of eight months or longer in employment or coverage.

   Karen was very unhappy with her job. She had a good lead for another one and decided to resign in January. However, negotiations fell apart, and in November, the company withdrew its offer. Karen decided it was time to retire. However, she would not qualify for a Part B SEP because she had a gap of nine months. (Her SEP started February 1 and ended September 30.)

There are two different enrollment procedures: one for those not enrolled in Medicare and a second for those enrolled in Part A. Chapter 4, "Over 65: Enrolling in Medicare," will discuss those procedures.

Questions and Answers about the Part B SEP

Is there an SEP for Part A enrollment?

No, there isn't. That's because, if you're eligible for premium-free Part A but didn't enroll at age 65, you can do that at any time. Here's an example.

> A large company changed its benefits, and hospitalization now has a very high deductible. Part A might help cover that. Those with that employer group plan can enroll in Part A now and continue to delay Part B enrollment until retirement.

If you are retiring and need to enroll in both Part A and Part B, you can do that during the Part B SEP.

If I have an eight-month SEP to enroll in Part B after retirement, why do you recommend I do it right away?

If you enroll during the SEP, you won't miss your chance or face any late enrollment penalties. However, there is a bigger risk. Coverage after age 65 not related to employment becomes secondary to Medicare. Without Part A and Part B, the secondary payer would have nothing to pay.

Here are two examples of language in retiree plan documents that emphasize the importance of not delaying enrollment.

> This example comes from an East Coast state plan information: "*If you fail to enroll in Medicare* or are still in a waiting period for Medicare to go into effect, you will be responsible for hospital and

medical expenses that Medicare would have covered if you had enrolled on a timely basis."

Here's language from a retiree plan: "If the retiree and covered dependents *fail to enroll in Medicare Parts A and B*, the member will be responsible for the Medicare portion (about 80 percent) of all eligible services."

To ensure that you have coverage, enroll as soon as possible.

What about the Part B SEP and those who work for a company with fewer than 20 employees?

Those who have a small EGHP and meet the criteria will qualify for a Part B SEP. However, by law, a small EGHP becomes secondary to Medicare. Delaying enrollment past age 65 can be risky and not something I would recommend. Here's why.

> Dennis works for a company with 15 employees. Two months before his 65th birthday, his boss told him he could continue with the company plan, so Dennis did not enroll in Medicare. A year later, he slipped in his shower and broke his hip. The insurer of the company group health plan said he should have enrolled in Medicare and refused to pay his medical expenses.

In this situation, Medicare is the primary payer. Because he had not enrolled, it is as though he had no insurance.

Dennis is still working and covered by a group health plan, so he qualifies for a Part B SEP. If he enrolls right away, he probably can have coverage in place next month, but that won't help with the expenses he has already incurred.

Will I qualify for a Part B SEP if I get one year of paid coverage as part of a severance package?

You will qualify if you enroll within the eight-month window that starts with the date your employment ends. If you wait until the end of the paid coverage, you won't. Remember, the date employment or coverage ends, whichever comes first, establishes the start of the eight-month SEP.

What happens if I don't qualify for a Part B SEP?

Your only option then will be to enroll during the GEP. Part B will be delayed, and you could face a late enrollment penalty.

The General Enrollment Period (GEP)

Unlike the IEP and the SEP, the GEP is for those who missed their first opportunity, and now there is a problem. There are three groups subject to the GEP.

- *Everyone over age 65 who does not have employer group coverage based on either their current employment or that of a spouse and did nothing during their IEP.*
  A retiree with a plan through his union or a self-employed carpenter with an individual plan will not have a Part B SEP. That's because this coverage is not sponsored by an employer.
- *Those who retired after age 65 but did not enroll during their eight-month SEP.*
  Usually, this happens because they have postemployment coverage, such as a COBRA or a retiree plan. If continuing with this coverage for more than eight months after their employment ended, they lose their chance to enroll during the SEP.
- *Those who do not qualify for premium-free Part A, hospital insurance, and did not enroll during the IEP.*

They (or a spouse) did not work and pay the appropriate taxes for 10 years. They are not eligible for premium-free Part A and should have enrolled during their IEP.

Because these groups did not enroll during their IEP and did not qualify for or take action during the Part B SEP, they must wait until the GEP. This period starts January 1 and ends March 31. Coverage will start the month after enrolling. For instance, enroll in February, and Medicare will start March 1. After enrolling in Medicare, there is an opportunity to pick a Medicare path and enroll in additional coverage. (See chap. 3, "The Two Medicare Paths.")

As if waiting until January isn't bad enough, there is another big problem: a late enrollment penalty applies if going more than one year (a full 12 months) without Part B, medical insurance. (See chap. 2, "Questions and Answers about the IEP.") Here's one example.

> Kevin was a personal trainer. He considered himself to be a perfect specimen of health and fitness and never thought about the fact that he was getting older. At age 68, he realized he hadn't enrolled in Medicare. His late enrollment penalty is for three years. In 2022 dollars, he paid an additional $51 every month.

Questions and Answers about the GEP

Why doesn't COBRA continuation coverage qualify me for an SEP?

COBRA is one of the biggest reasons why individuals miss the chance to enroll during their SEP. The coverage is the same as they had when working; it is sponsored by their (former) employer. Why should there be a problem?

Here's the difference with COBRA. The individual is no longer employed. The Part B SEP begins the first of the next month after their coverage or employment ends, whichever comes first. Continuing with COBRA for longer than eight months after their job ends puts them right into the GEP.

Are there any other repercussions associated with the GEP, besides the Part B late enrollment penalty?

There are two additional late enrollment situations.

- *There may be an issue with the prescription drug coverage.*
  Kevin, the personal trainer, didn't have any drug coverage, so he faced a late enrollment penalty for Part D. In 2022, his penalty added $11.90 every month. Just as with the Part B penalty, this amount can change every year and doesn't go away. (See chap. 2, "Questions and Answers about the IEP.")

- *Those who do not qualify for premium-free Part A will also face a late enrollment penalty.*
  If they don't purchase Part A when first eligible, they could pay 10 percent more in monthly premiums. They will have to pay the penalty for twice the number of years they didn't enroll. (See chap. 2, "Questions and Answers about the IEP.")

By now, you realize how important timing is to your Medicare decision. Here are your take-away tips.

1. Pay attention and determine what you need to do about Medicare during your IEP.
2. Enroll in Medicare during your Part B SEP if you delayed enrollment because you had an employer plan

       connected to the current employment of you or your spouse and that employment is now ending.

3. Do the right things during your IEP and SEP, and you won't have to deal with the GEP.

In the next chapter, you'll learn all about the parts and paths of Medicare.

Chapter 3

The Parts and Paths of Medicare

You've determined it's time for Medicare. Now what do you do? How do you know what to pick? You could watch the commercials and call the phone numbers. You could ask your best friend what works. You could let an agent put together your plan. Or you could take charge of one of your most important decisions. You're reading this book, which means you're ready to do that.

We have all been taught that Medicare has four parts—A, B, C, and D. So many of us believe that when we tackle Medicare, we need to get an A, a B, a C, and a D. Unfortunately, that is where I think Medicare confusion begins.

As you look at the coverage you'll need going forward with Medicare, there are three essential parts, and they combine into packages, which I call paths. Let's begin with an introduction to the parts of Medicare.

The Three Parts of Medicare and Costs Overview

Part A, Hospital Insurance

This part covers four important services.

- *Inpatient hospitalization:* This coverage applies when an individual is admitted to the hospital, on a doctor's order, for the treatment of an illness or injury.

- *Skilled nursing facility (SNF) stay:* This is generally post-hospital care provided in a Medicare-certified nursing home or as part of a hospital. The patient needs specialized, daily care that requires the skills of a nurse, such as intravenous administration or complex wound care, or a therapist, like those needed for rehabilitation after a car crash or stroke. About 5 percent of Medicare beneficiaries qualify for a skilled stay, with an average length of 25 days.
- *Home health care:* A nurse or therapist from a Medicare-certified home health agency visits a home to provide skilled care. Usually, care is intermittent, meaning not daily. The patient must be homebound or confined to the home due to medical reasons.
- *Hospice:* A Medicare-certified hospice provides multidisciplinary end-of-life care to a beneficiary with a life expectancy of less than than six months. This is palliative or comfort, not curative, care.

Part A is premium-free for those who worked and paid Medicare taxes for at least 10 years (40 quarters) and earned 40 credits or whose spouse did. Those who do not have enough credits can purchase Part A. (See chap. 7, "Premiums for Medicare Coverage.")

Part B, Medical Insurance
Think of this as the outpatient component of Medicare. There are two types of services.

1. *Medically necessary services to diagnose and treat a medical condition:* These include physician services, diagnostic tests, and any care or treatment that can be provided in an outpatient setting, such as physical therapy, day surgery, or radiation treatments.
2. *Preventive services:* At the top of the list are the annual flu shots, pneumonia vaccinations, and the COVID vaccine

and boosters. Important preventive services for women include mammograms and pelvic exams; for men, PSA (prostate-specific antigen) tests and prostate exams; and for everyone, the beloved colonoscopy. Most of these services have no copayment.

As you learned in the previous chapter, Part B is optional insurance. Those who have coverage through an employer group health plan (EGHP) connected to the current employment of the individual or spouse can defer enrollment. It is optional because this part comes with a standard monthly premium, $170.10 in 2022. Higher-income beneficiaries will pay more. (See chap. 7, "IRMAA.")

Part D, Prescription Drug Coverage

Private insurance companies, not Medicare, administer this coverage. The name of the insurance company will likely appear in the plan's name. Here are some important points to know about prescription drug coverage.

- There are about 20–23 stand-alone plans available to almost everyone.
- A Part D stand-alone drug plan helps to cover the cost of prescription medications listed in its formulary (list of covered drugs). These plans charge monthly premiums and usually have deductibles. There is also cost sharing (copayments and coinsurance).
- The physician must write an order. If you can get a drug OTC (over the counter) at a drugstore without an order, Part D won't pay for it.
- Medicare sets some basic standards that every drug plan must follow. Plans must cover all drugs in certain categories. Then each plan must cover at least two in the other categories. As a result, every plan likely has a different formulary, its list of covered drugs. (See chap. 6, "Part D, Prescription Drug Coverage.")

As with Part B, this is optional insurance. Those who have some other creditable drug coverage, such as with a retiree plan, can put off getting a Part D plan. (See chap. 2, "Identify Your Situation.")

What happened to Part C? Part C is Medicare Advantage. This isn't really a part but rather is a package of the three essential parts, Part A, Part B, and Part D. In one of its publications, Medicare says, "Medicare Advantage, sometimes called Part C, is an all-in-one alternative to Original Medicare (Part A and Part B)." That's why I never refer to Medicare Advantage as Part C. I think it was called Part C initially because someone in charge of Medicare saw a hole in the alphabet of parts and decided to fill it by labeling Medicare Advantage as Part C. You'll learn more about this in chapter 3, "The Two Medicare Paths."

Medicare Costs and the Need for Additional Coverage

You could enroll in Part A and Part B, get a Part D drug plan, and be done. You would have Medicare coverage for hospitalization, outpatient care, and medications, with no penalties. Plus, you might save money on additional premiums. However, you better have a lot more money saved because you'll need it if you get sick. Part A and Part B come with many out-of-pocket costs that you would have to pay. These were the 2022 costs. (See www.dianeomdahl.com/updates for updated information.)

Part A, hospital insurance
- Hospital deductible: $1,556 per benefit period.
- Extended hospitalizations: $389 for days 61–90 in a benefit period, and $778 per day for days 90–150 (lifetime reserve days). (See chap. 6, "Questions and Answers about Part A and Part B Services.")
- SNF: $194.50 per day for days 21–100.
- Hospice: 5 percent coinsurance for inpatient respite stays and hospice-related medications.

Part B, medical insurance

- Deductible: $233.
- 20 percent coinsurance (of the Medicare-approved amount) after meeting the deductible.
- Part B excess charges (physicians who do not accept Medicare assignment, usually specialists, can charge up to 15 percent more than Medicare approves). (See chap. 6, "Part B, Medical Insurance.")

Part A or Part B, depending on care setting

- First three pints of blood (if the provider has to purchase the blood).

Because of these unlimited costs, additional coverage of some kind becomes so important in situations such as this one.

> Russell was a very healthy 72-year-old farmer and rarely needed medical care. But then he started having stomach problems. In fall 2022, he saw a doctor who ordered a slew of tests. In no time, he met the Part B deductible (the first $233 of outpatient costs). The tests showed a tumor and the diagnosis was cancer. He had surgery (a hospitalization deductible of $1,556) and chemotherapy treatments (20 percent of the cost). And with Part A and Part B, there is no cap or limit on how much he must pay.

After enrolling in Part A and Part B, some beneficiaries have other options—such as COBRA, retiree coverage, TRICARE for Life, or a Federal Employee Health Benefits (FEHB) plan—that can protect against unlimited out-of-pocket costs. (These unique situations have different rules and risks that we'll address in chapter 3, "Know When You Need More Help.")

Questions and Answers about the Parts and Costs of Medicare

Is Part B a supplement?

A Medigap policy is a supplement.

However, many do think of Part B as supplemental insurance. Without it, you would not have coverage for outpatient services, so it is an essential part of Medicare.

There is a valid reason for this confusion. In the 1960s, when Medicare became law, Part B was called Supplementary Medical Insurance. That's likely because medical care was hospital-based. Outpatient departments were very small and mostly for doctors' appointments. Then as medical care shifted to outpatient delivery, Part B services became more important, and Medicare Supplement Insurance (Medigap policies) came into being. Somewhere along the line, *supplementary* eased out of the everyday title, and Medicare.gov now refers to Part B as medical insurance.

Will Medicare cover medical care outside of the United States?

For Original Medicare, Part A and Part B only, the answer is generally no, except in very limited situations. Many Medigap plans offer a foreign travel emergency benefit. There are some Medicare Advantage plans that provide foreign travel benefits. Look into the plan's Evidence of Coverage (EOC), or talk with a plan representative about what a plan may cover. (Learn more in chapter 6, "Other Coverage Concerns.")

If I don't take any prescription medications, do I have to get Part D drug coverage?

Part D coverage is optional, but consider these points.

- You never know what's around the corner. If you need to take medications and don't have drug coverage, you would be responsible for the full cost.
- If you change your mind and want to add Part D coverage later on, you could only do this at designated times. During the Open Enrollment Period (OEP), October 15–December 7, you can enroll in a Part D drug plan or a Medicare Advantage plan with drug coverage. (See chap. 8, "Changing Plans.")
- If you go without drug coverage for more than two months, you face a Part D late enrollment penalty.

This situation demonstrates the importance of getting drug coverage when you're first eligible.

> Lisa was extremely healthy. She ran marathons, had no significant medical history, and was the envy of her friends. At age 65, she enrolled in Medicare but did not get a drug plan. Then in February, right before her 73rd birthday, she was diagnosed with an arthritic condition. Her physician began treating her with an inexpensive drug. A few months later, they both knew this was not working, and she tried other medications. In August, she started on a biologic drug. Without Part D coverage, Lisa was responsible for the full price of her drugs that year, over $5,000.
>
> Lisa enrolled in a drug plan during the OEP in 2021 so she would have coverage going forward. But then she found out about the penalty. Because she was without drug coverage for 106 months, she paid an additional $35 every month in 2022. (See chap. 2, "Questions and Answers about the IEP.")

The Two Medicare Paths

Because you don't want to be hit with unlimited out-of-pocket costs, you're going to need something to help keep you out of bankruptcy. It's time to meet the paths of Medicare. For most people, the three parts of Medicare (Part A, Part B, and Part D) combine into two paths, providing comprehensive coverage and controlled costs.

- *The Original Medicare Path:* This starts with Part A, hospital insurance, and Part B, medical insurance, and then adds two essential pieces of coverage.
  1. Medicare Supplement Insurance is commonly called a Medigap policy because it helps to cover the gaps in Medicare coverage. (This book uses the terms "Medicare supplement" and "Medigap policy" interchangeably.) This is coverage sponsored by private insurance companies that works with Part A and Part B.
  2. A stand-alone Part D prescription drug plan (PDP) helps to cover prescription medications.
- *The Medicare Advantage Path:* Medicare labeled this coverage as Part C, but I rarely use that title. Medicare Advantage is really the three parts of Medicare (Part A, Part B, and Part D) put together in one package. Private insurance companies administer this insurance.

What's the best way to understand the two Medicare paths? Picture yourself hiking in the country. Turn your head one way, and the path heads toward the mountains. Turn the other way, and the path winds down to the river. These are two separate and distinct paths that raise questions. How will your journey go? How much will it cost? What are the rules? If you take one path, how easy will it be to change your mind and go the other way?

These two paths, Original Medicare and Medicare Advantage, cover 60 percent of beneficiaries. Each path is a viable option, but everyone's situation is different. Before taking your first step, you need to know about where you're heading and the traveling conditions.

Original Medicare Path

Let's start with the Original Medicare Path, the one that has been around the longest.

This path is administered by the federal government. Health care providers must know and follow Medicare rules and criteria. There is no insurance company between patients and doctors. Here's what that means to you.

- There are no provider networks, no HMOs (health maintenance organizations) or PPOs (preferred provider organizations). Instead, you will deal with doctors and providers that accept Medicare assignment. These providers go through a process to register with Medicare. They don't have to see every Medicare patient, but for the ones they see, they must submit claims to Medicare and cannot charge any more than Medicare allows. In return, they get paid directly from Medicare.
- You won't need referrals to see any physicians.
- Your physicians are in charge of your care and treatment. For just about all medical care under Original Medicare, there are no prior authorization requirements.

  > Sherry sprained her ankle. She could start physical therapy immediately because her physician did not need to get approval from the insurance company.

- The Original Medicare Path will travel with you around the country. If you need medical care anywhere in the

United States or its territories, check the Physician Compare database to find health care providers.

Here's how to find doctors who will accept Medicare assignment.

1. Go to the Physician Compare database at www.medicare-links.com/physician-compare.
2. Look for the words "charges the Medicare-approved amount."

The Original Medicare Path starts with Part A and Part B. As noted previously, there is no limit on out-of-pocket costs. In addition to these parts, two types of coverage can protect your pocketbook and enhance your coverage.

1. A Part D stand-alone drug plan is administered by a private insurance company, not Medicare. (Usually, the insurance company's name is in the title of the plan.)
   - No matter where you live, there are stand-alone drug plans available.
   - A drug plan helps cover the cost of prescription medications in its formulary (list of covered drugs).
2. A Medigap policy is managed by a private insurance company.
   - There are many companies that sell these policies. For instance, on its website, the Wisconsin insurance commissioner lists 27 Medigap insurers licensed to sell policies.
   - This policy helps cover the gaps in Part A and Part B, those costs that Medicare doesn't pay. For example, any policy must cover the Part B 20 percent coinsurance.

- Medigap policies in 10 states are standardized by letters. Each letter represents a package of benefits and costs. Massachusetts, Minnesota, and Wisconsin have their own models, but the policies work the same way.
- You pay a monthly premium for a Medigap policy.
- Medigap premiums can go up every year. Understanding how these policies are priced can help mitigate the impact of those increases.
- Learn more about the plans, benefits, and pricing in chapter 5, "Shopping for a Medigap Policy."

Think of the Original Medicare Path as a "pay-now approach." You'll pay monthly premiums for a set package of benefits, as designated by a letter. Then you'll face predictable out-of-pocket costs. Plan F policyholders who see doctors participating in Medicare do not get any bills. Those with Plan G would only pay the Part B deductible.

Medicare Advantage Path

You've probably seen at least one commercial with a football MVP or TV celebrity promoting Medicare Advantage. These commercials hit the hot spots like no premiums, extra benefits, and money back. The goal is to get you to call the number on the screen and enroll. What the commercials say is true; however, what they leave unsaid can have an impact on your path decision, one you may have to live with for the rest of your life. You need to give this choice the same consideration you did when choosing your career or partner. (Although it's possible the Medicare Advantage decision may be even more permanent.) (See chap. 3, "Changing Paths down the Road.")

Private insurance companies manage Medicare Advantage plans, so there will be an insurance company name as part of the title. According to the Kaiser Family Foundation, there were 39 plans available to the average beneficiary in 2022.

Medicare Advantage plans must provide the same Part A and Part B services that Original Medicare covers, but plans can set the rules and determine how to operate. There are four coverage rules of consequence.

1. You may have to receive services in a network—that is, a group of doctors, other health care providers, hospitals, and facilities under contract with the plan.
   - Some plans, particularly HMOs, will cover routine, or nonemergency, care from in-network providers only.
   - Other plans, like PPOs, give the flexibility to choose providers out-of-network without a referral. However, know two important points.
     1. You may pay more for this coverage, such as $25 for a specialist in-network and $50 for one out-of-network. Or the plan may charge $335 a day for the first six days of hospitalization in-network but 35 percent of the cost for an out-of-network stay.
     2. You can choose your physicians, but those physicians have no obligation to see patients that are not in their contracted networks.
   - These networks can change every year, and sometimes during the year, so you may have to find new physicians.
2. You may need a referral or written order from your primary doctor to see specialists and other health care providers.
3. A plan can require prior approval or prior authorization of certain services. Before you can receive treatment, the insurance company has to review your case and determine what it will cover. Your treatment could be delayed by the review, possibly limited or denied. (See chap. 3, "Questions and Answers about Medicare Paths.")

Here are some other things to know about Advantage plans.

- There are several types of plans. The two most popular plans are an HMO and a PPO. (Learn about other plans in chapter 5, "Shopping for a Medicare Advantage Plan.")
- Most plans include prescription drug coverage, so you don't need to purchase a stand-alone Part D drug plan.
- Plans can provide additional benefits that Medicare doesn't cover, like dental, vision, and hearing.
  - Again, there are rules and limits. A plan may cover only preventive services, such as cleaning and X-rays, or impose a dollar cap on services. You may have to use in-network providers.
  - A word of caution: Don't let the extra benefits that are available be the primary driver of your decision. The medical care that you need is more important.
- For the last few years, plans have been able to offer daily maintenance benefits, such as transportation, meals, and personal aide services.
  - These are long-term care (LTC) services that Medicare doesn't cover. Not every plan provides these benefits, and again, there are limits. You can get 30 roundtrips for medical care or a private home aide for up to four hours a day for 30 days in a year.
  - Plans can also limit the number of benefits you choose in a calendar year.
- Medicare Advantage uses a "pay-as-you-go" approach.
  - Plans have no or low premiums, but there is cost sharing (deductibles, copayments, and co-insurance) for most services.
  - You are protected by an out-of-pocket maximum, the most you will pay in a calendar year.

Write checks until you reach that limit, and the plan covers everything for the rest of the year. The limit resets as of January 1.

○ Medicare set the maximum limit plans can charge at $7,550 for in-network care and $11,300 for in- and out-of-network combined. Plans can offer lower limits.

Questions and Answers about the Medicare Paths

Do I have to enroll in Part B to get a Medicare Advantage plan?

Some believe they can skip the Part B premium if they elect Medicare Advantage. But that's a misbelief. You must have both Part A and Part B to qualify for either a Medicare Advantage plan or a Medigap policy.

How difficult is it to find doctors who accept assignment?

You may recall seeing headlines several years ago that doctors were dropping out of Medicare. The problem started in 1997, when the Balanced Budget Act tried to control the Medicare spending growth rate for physicians. However, the formula would have resulted in cuts to physicians, and as expected, there were many protests. For the next 17 years, Congress applied temporary legislation that basically kicked the can down the road. Finally, in 2015, new legislation, known as the "Doc Fix," remedied these problems by focusing on value-based payments, rewarding physicians who perform well under the new systems, and penalizing those who perform poorly.

According to the Kaiser Family Foundation, 99 percent of doctors in the United States accept Medicare assignment. Of that group, 71 percent are seeing new patients.

Does a physician assistant accept Medicare assignment?

If you choose the Original Medicare Path, you can continue to see your physician assistant. That's because this practitioner is on the list of those who are required to accept assignment; along with nurse practitioners, clinical psychologists, and clinical social workers. There are other practitioners on that list, so always ask whether your providers accept assignment.

Can you explain prior authorization?

Many Medicare Advantage plans require prior approval of certain services. These include inpatient admissions, SNF stays, mental health services, home health care, chiropractic services, outpatient surgery and services, ambulance transport, medical equipment, diagnostic tests, and laboratory and radiology services.

In the case of a procedure or test, the plan will either approve or deny the request. For services such as outpatient therapy or home health care, if the plan approves the order, it will likely specify a certain number of visits. Getting more visits than that will require additional approval.

It is the responsibility of the member to know the plan's requirements and to ensure that services are authorized.

Promotional information for plans likely will not mention this requirement. But be aware. In 2020, 99 percent of Medicare Advantage members were in plans that required prior authorization for some services, up from 80 percent in 2018.

What happens if I have a procedure without authorization?

If the procedure is not authorized, the Medicare Advantage plan likely will not pay. In a plan's EOC, there is language saying something like, "While a provider will generally make these requests and submit the necessary forms, it is a member's responsibility to make certain the process is followed."

You are ultimately responsible to ensure that the necessary care is authorized.

> Last year, my business got a call from Gail. She had a knee replacement for bone-on-bone osteoarthritis. She has no idea what happened, but the authorization was never processed. Now she got a bill for $60,000. Her plan would not pay because the procedure was not authorized and said that Gail should have known the rules.

Does the Original Medicare Path have any prior authorization requirements?

For most services, like physician visits, hospitalizations, and outpatient care, no authorization is required. Your physician writes an order, and your treatment can start.

However, there are a few times when your providers will have to get approval from Medicare. Certain types of power mobility devices require authorization because of concerns about inappropriate use. Procedures that could be considered cosmetic, such as varicose vein surgery or breast reduction, can also require authorization to confirm that they are medically necessary.

Isn't a zero-premium plan too good to true?

There are zero-premium Medicare Advantage plans available to most Medicare beneficiaries. However, a plan with no premium does not mean it's free. You may not pay for visits with your primary doctor, but you could write checks for diagnostic studies, hospitalizations, specialists, and outpatient care.

So go beyond the premium to how much you may ultimately have to pay, the plan's maximum out-of-pocket limit. Also investigate other important points, like the network and coverage rules.

Why did Medicare raise the maximum limits for Medicare Advantage plans?

In 2011, Medicare set the maximum out-of-pocket limit for in-network services to $6,700 and $10,000 for in- and out-of-network combined. But in 2021, those limits increased to $7,550 and $11,300.

The impetus behind the change is mainly one condition. Since the beginning of Medicare Advantage plans, individuals diagnosed with end-stage renal disease (ESRD), or kidney failure, have not been able to enroll in an Advantage plan. If they were already in a plan and then were diagnosed, they could keep it. But now those who have ESRD can enroll in a Medicare Advantage plan. Because these beneficiaries typically incur higher costs, the limits for everyone increased.

How many people really hit those new maximum limits?

I have never found any studies addressing this, so I don't have an answer. Rather, I look at the maximum limits as a planning tool. In a worst-case scenario, you would need to pay those costs.

Consider a person who is diagnosed with cancer or who needs dialysis. Most plans charge a straight 20 percent for these treatments, and more if you go out-of-network. Reaching that limit is a real possibility when you need these treatments.

Are drug costs generally less in a Medicare Advantage plan than a stand-alone drug plan?

Sometimes you'll pay less with a Medicare Advantage plan, and sometimes you won't. Your costs all depend on your medications and the coverage you choose.

How much you might pay for drugs now shouldn't be a big concern in picking your path. Drug coverage, be it a stand-alone Part D plan or a Medicare Advantage plan that includes

Part D coverage, changes every year, and so may your drugs. During the OEP, you have the opportunity to check other plans and find new coverage. However, you may not be able to change your path every year. (See chap. 3, "Changing Paths down the Road.")

What kind of coverage should I get if I spend four or five months every year at a vacation home?

Both paths, Original Medicare and Medicare Advantage, will cover emergency care at your vacation home. However, spending significant time in a different location means you need to investigate what you'll do in case you need non-emergency care, possibly for a bad case of the flu or a painful sprain.

If considering Original Medicare,

- check the status of providers you would like to see in the Physician Compare database,
- determine whether they are accepting new patients, and
- know that a Medigap policy will work with Part A and Part B, no matter where you are in the United States.

If you choose Medicare Advantage,

- consider a plan that would cover out-of-network services (see chap. 5, "Shopping for a Medicare Advantage Plan"),
- if the plan offers out-of-network coverage, you won't need referrals, but confirm that the providers you want to see will bill your plan,
- then check your costs, especially the out-of-pocket maximum, for out-of-network care, and
- know that the plan you select this year may change next year.

Wesley and his wife chose a Medicare Advantage plan that listed about 40 select counties around the country in-network (including the one where their vacation home was). That worked fine for three years, and then the plan dropped that county from the network. They couldn't find a similar replacement plan, and now they will pay out-of-network rates for any nonemergency services at their vacation home.

Changing Paths down the Road

There are many factors to consider before you choose your Medicare path. One of the most important, yet seldom discussed until it is too late, is whether and when you can change your path. Generally, this is not something you're going to do unless things just haven't worked out as you thought. Perhaps you're having difficulty getting the care you need or you're paying too much. Can you switch from the Medicare Advantage Path back to the Original Medicare Path or vice versa? If so, when and how? The answers depend on many factors, so let's look at the different scenarios.

Changing from the Medicare Advantage Path to the Original Medicare Path

You're just getting into Medicare. You may consider yourself healthy. Maybe you see a doctor only once or twice a year. Or, if you have health issues, you're not going to spend enough to hit the maximum limit for several years. You really could use the dental, vision, and fitness benefits. Why should you pay premiums for a Medigap policy (Medicare supplement plan) and Part D drug plan when you can get a zero-premium Medicare Advantage plan? Then when you start having medical problems, you can drop that plan and get a Medigap policy and drug plan, right?

The answer is maybe, maybe not. Before making a decision, you must know about the impact of preexisting conditions on your ability to purchase a Medigap policy.

Guaranteed Issue Right

A preexisting condition is a health problem—like heart disease, diabetes, or cancer—that you had before the date that new health coverage starts. These conditions can lead to a denial of your application for a Medigap policy. If you do qualify, your medical history could mean higher premiums.

However, this is where guaranteed issue right comes into play. If you have one, a Medigap insurance company cannot deny your application for a policy or charge higher premiums because of any preexisting medical conditions. Those enrolling in Medicare Part B for the first time, either at age 65 or later on when retiring, will have a six-month guaranteed issue right. This is known as the Medigap Open Enrollment Period, a six-month period that begins on the effective date for Part B, medical insurance. Here's how it works.

> Juan enrolled in Part A, hospital insurance, at age 65. Three years later, he retired and enrolled in Part B, which took effect January 1, 2022. His Medigap Open Enrollment Period began January 1 and ended June 30. He purchased his Medigap policy in February with no medical questions.

If Juan had delayed applying for a Medigap policy and his six-month window closed, he would no longer have had a guaranteed issue right. The Medigap insurer could have applied medical underwriting, and his application could have been denied.

> ## Facts about the Medigap Open Enrollment Period
>
> - This is a six-month period that begins automatically when Part B takes effect.
> - Once this period begins, it cannot be changed or restarted. You only get one.

What about if you opt for a Medicare Advantage plan when Part B first takes effect? Everyone has a guaranteed issue right during this period. That window closes in six months, and then the right disappears; you get only one bite at the apple. However, there can be a guaranteed issue right in other circumstances.

Four States

If you live in Connecticut, Massachusetts, or New York, you're eligible for continuous open enrollment for Medigap policies. That means Medigap insurance companies must sell a Medigap policy at any time to any eligible beneficiary (enrolled in Part A and Part B), regardless of age or health status. Companies cannot charge higher premiums because of preexisting conditions.

Those living in Maine have an annual guaranteed issue right to get Medigap Plan A. (See chap. 5, "Shopping for a Medigap Policy.")

You may be able to apply for a Medigap policy at any time, but you can only drop a Medicare Advantage plan during one of the OEPs. (See chap. 8, "Changing Plans.")

Trial Periods

You wouldn't buy a new car without a test-drive, so it's good to know that's available for Medicare Advantage. Two trial periods provide a risk-free opportunity to test how this coverage would work for you.

1. *Electing Medicare Advantage during your Initial Enrollment Period (IEP).*
   - If you enroll in a Medicare Advantage plan at age 65, when initially eligible for Medicare, you have a 12-month trial period.
   - At any time during the first 12 months after the plan takes effect, you can disenroll from, or drop, the Medicare Advantage plan and return to Original Medicare Part A and Part B and get a Part D drug plan.
   - You will also have a guaranteed issue right to get a Medigap policy, no matter your health status or state of residence. You can purchase any Medigap policy that's sold in your state by any insurance company.

   Linda turned 65 in November 2022 and enrolled in a Medicare Advantage plan. Her trial period began November 1 and would end October 31, 2023.
   She had "buyer's remorse" eight months later and decided to drop the plan, effective June 30. Her Original Medicare coverage began July 1, and she got a Medigap policy.

2. *Dropping a Medigap policy after age 65 to enroll in a Medicare Advantage plan.*
   - Perhaps you start out with Original Medicare and a Medicare supplement plan, but later on, you want to try a Medicare Advantage plan.
   - You would have a 12-month trial period, which begins on the effective date of coverage for the Medicare Advantage plan.
   - You have the right to buy back the same Medigap policy that was in effect before enrolling in the Medicare Advantage plan, if the company still sells it.
   - If your former Medigap policy isn't available, you can buy any Medigap plan that's sold in your state

by any insurance company, except Plan M and Plan N.

- This trial applies only the first time you give up the Medigap policy.
- This trial period also applies to residents of Massachusetts, Minnesota, and Wisconsin. Check the state health insurance website for more details.

Caution: With both these trial periods, you must disenroll before the end of the 12th month. If you don't, your next opportunity would be during the OEP or the Medicare Advantage OEP. Then you may not have a guaranteed issue right to get a Medigap policy, so you would likely have to pass medical underwriting.

Check Out Your State's Medigap Requirements

The federal government has established requirements for Medigap policies. All policies must:

- be identified as Medicare Supplement Insurance,
- honor beneficiary protections and rights, and
- follow state laws.

It is the last one that causes the significant variations in policies and rules from state to state.

This book focuses on the federal requirements for Medigap policies and highlights the more significant state-specific issues, like birthday rules. You may have to check your state's insurance commissioner website or talk with a knowledgeable agent about specific concerns.

As with so many issues related to Medigap policies, there can be variations depending on the state of residence and the insurance company. For example, Maine offers a three-year Medicare Advantage trial period, and some insurance companies offer extended trial periods. Your plan options may also be different from the federal law specifications. *Important:* Check your state's health insurance website or plan information for details before making any changes.

Specific Circumstances

There are times, outside of a trial period, when Medicare Advantage plan members can drop this coverage and choose Original Medicare. They can get a drug plan and will have a guaranteed issue right to get a Medigap policy. These situations are very specific and, most of them, not all that common. Here are three that happen more frequently.

- Circumstances dictate a move out of the plan's service area.

  After the death of her husband, Sandra moved from Florida back to Wisconsin. Her family decided that the Original Medicare Path would be best for her then.

- Changes in health status necessitate a move into or out of an SNF.

  Glenn had a stroke and required care that could not be provided in his home. The facility he wanted was not in any network, so he decided to switch paths to Original Medicare.

- The Medicare Advantage plan's contract is not renewed.

  Rita's plan decided to exit her market. She did not want any of the other plans and opted for the Original Medicare Path.

The time frame for making the change depends on the situation. If you have questions, contact Medicare or check out Medicare.gov.

The Medicare.gov website lists four ways to disenroll from a Medicare Advantage plan.

- Call (800) 633-4227 (MEDICARE).
- Mail or fax a signed written notice to the plan telling them you want to disenroll.
- Submit a request to the plan online, if that option is available.
- Ask the plan to send a disenrollment notice that you can complete and send back to the insurance company.

What can you do if you want to drop your Medicare Advantage plan and you don't fall into any of these situations? You can disenroll from the plan during the OEP or the Medicare Advantage OEP. You will return to Part A and Part B and can enroll in a Part D drug plan. Depending on your state of residence and health status, you may have to pass medical underwriting to get a Medigap policy. There may be no guarantee, but you could still qualify for one.

Changing from the Original Medicare Path to Medicare Advantage

If you have Original Medicare with a Medigap policy and Part D drug plan, switching to Medicare Advantage is much easier than going the other way. That's because Medicare Advantage plans cannot subject applicants to medical underwriting. A plan must accept any eligible beneficiary—that is, one who is enrolled in Part A and Part B and lives in the plan's service area.

To navigate this switch, simply choose an Advantage plan and enroll in it during the OEP, beginning in October, and then you will be dropped from the Original Medicare Part A and Part B and the drug coverage. You must notify the Medigap insurer so the premium bills will stop.

Questions and Answers about Changing Paths

What is medical underwriting?

This is a process used by insurance companies to determine your health status when applying for health insurance coverage. The application will ask questions about smoking habits, medical history, medications you take, and any upcoming surgical procedures or treatments. The companies then factor these conditions into your eligibility to get a plan, what you will pay, and the coverage you'll have.

Medicare supplements can apply medical underwriting; Medicare Advantage plans cannot.

Didn't the Affordable Care Act (ACA) eliminate a plan's ability to deny coverage because of preexisting conditions?

Yes, the ACA eliminated medical underwriting for new enrollees in the individual market and some other situations. But many other types of coverage can still utilize medical underwriting, including Medigap policies. That's why figuring out what to do during your six-month Medigap Open Enrollment Period is so important.

If I have a guaranteed issue right, can a Medigap insurer ever delay the start of coverage?

The insurer cannot make you wait for the policy to start. However, they can make you wait for coverage of a preexisting condition. Aptly named a "preexisting condition waiting period," this can be up to six months with no payment from the Medigap policy for the condition(s). The policy can delay payment if:

- a condition was treated or diagnosed within six months prior to purchasing the policy during the Medigap Open Enrollment Period, and
- you did not have continuous creditable coverage for at least six months before the Medigap policy started.

There are some important points to know about this waiting period.

- Creditable coverage is generally any other health coverage you recently had before applying for a Medigap policy. According to Healthcare.gov, this coverage can be a group health plan, individual health insurance, Medicaid, CHAMPUS, TRICARE, or an FEHB program plan, to name a few.
- If you end up with a waiting period, Part A and Part B will still cover Medicare's share of the bill. You will have to pay the copayments or coinsurance for the treatment of the preexisting condition.
- There is no waiting period for coverage of a new problem or one that was not treated during the six-month lookback period.
- After six months, the Medigap policy will pay its share for the treatment of the preexisting condition.

What are my chances of getting a Medigap policy if I don't have a guaranteed issue right?

That depends on several factors.

- Your health status: Conditions such as cancer, heart disease, osteoporosis, diabetes, or Alzheimer's disease often lead to denials.
- Your medical history: A treated and resolved condition—like cancer, stroke, or a heart attack five years ago—could cause problems.

- The company with which you apply: Some insurers are more liberal. There is one national company in a midwestern state that will accept any applicant. The premiums may be more than some other plans, but there is no medical underwriting.
- The insurer's criteria: The best way to describe this is with an example.

> Dick had a rare medical condition, an automatic disqualifying condition for most insurers. However, he dug into the small print of many policies. He identified one company that did not ask questions about that condition on its application.

You may not have a guaranteed issue right, but it still may be possible to get a policy. You never know until you try. If you are unable to qualify for a Medigap policy, you can enroll in a Medicare Advantage plan. There is no medical underwriting.

Wil I be able to get a Medigap policy when I give up my small employer plan?

If you work for a company with fewer than 20 employees and you are able to continue with the group health plan once you turn 65, you should enroll in Medicare Part A and Part B. By law, Medicare becomes the primary payer. (See chap. 2, "Identify Your Situation.")

If you continue with this plan for more than six months, your Medigap Open Enrollment Period with a guaranteed issue right is gone. However, because you had to enroll in Medicare to have complete coverage, you will have an opportunity to get a Medigap policy. This special enrollment period with a guaranteed issue right generally lasts for 63 days after the employment or group health coverage ends.

How come I don't have a guaranteed issue right if I enroll in Part B and keep my large employer plan?

As you read in the previous question, those who keep a small employer plan after age 65 will get a 63-day guaranteed issue right to get a Medigap policy when retiring. However, that opportunity does not apply to those who enroll in Part B and keep a large employer plan.

The big difference is that a small employer plan becomes secondary to Medicare after age 65. Those employees are sort of forced to enroll in Medicare Part A and Part B if they want complete coverage. That is not the case with large employer plans. By law, a group plan sponsored by a company with 20 or more employees is primary to Medicare; it will continue to pay, even for those who don't enroll in Part A and Part B. Plus, the company cannot force employees to enroll in Medicare. If these employees do enroll in Part B, the day it takes effect starts the Medigap Open Enrollment Period clock. When that clock hits six months, the guaranteed issue right is gone.

Making Your Medicare Path Decision

By now, you should realize your Medicare path choice is very important. Don't choose coverage based solely on TV commercials, what works for a friend, or your agent's recommendations. Be selfish; make the decision for yourself.

As you work through all this, remember these important points.

- No matter your health status or where you live, you have a guaranteed issue right to get a Medicare supplement plan (Medigap policy) for the first six months you are enrolled in Part B.
- There is a Medicare Advantage trial period for those who elect this coverage when turning 65.

- If you live in Connecticut, Maine, Massachusetts, or New York, your path choice may not be a lifetime decision. You have the ability to change paths without your medical history having an impact.

Last-Minute Homework

Calculate Your Maximum Medicare Exposure

I used to help clients calculate their expected medical costs in a year—doctors' visits, hospitalizations, or whatever else. That was tedious and difficult because my crystal ball was broken. Then, realizing that many seniors don't want to face risk, I started focusing on the most they could possibly pay in a year. For lack of a better title, I dubbed this "Your Maximum Medicare Exposure."

Let's say you have an unexpectedly bad year, a medical tsunami with hospitalizations, specialist appointments, tests, and rehabilitation. Could you pay for the medical care during that year? Simply calculate your monthly premium plus your possible share of the out-of-pocket costs (the checks you write).

Here's an example for the Original Medicare Path with a Medigap Plan G (the fastest-growing supplement). A monthly premium comes with predictable out-of-pocket costs.

> Susan's monthly Medigap premium is $224. Her only cost sharing is the Part B deductible. Her maximum exposure in 2022 was $2,688 premiums + the Part B deductible ($233) = $2,921. No matter what happened, if she saw Medicare providers, she would have paid no more than $2,921.

A Medicare Advantage plan has no or low premiums and a maximum limit. Check out these two examples.

Steve lives in California and has an HMO plan with no monthly premium. His maximum Medicare exposure is $1,299, the plan's out-of-pocket maximum.

His sister, who lives down the block, pays a monthly premium of $90 for her PPO plan and the maximum limit is $6,700 in-network and $11,300 in- and out-of-network combined. Her maximum Medicare exposure is $7,780 if she stays in-network and $12,380 if she doesn't.

Remember, other considerations come into play—physician choice, coverage rules, extra benefits—but maximum exposure is a quick way to determine your financial risk.

Original Medicare Path
Here's the homework if you are considering the Original Medicare Path.

Physicians
- Check the status of your doctors in the Physician Compare database at www.medicare-links.com/medicare-plan-finder.

Travel
- Look for physicians and providers around your travel destinations within the United States.
- Find a Medigap policy that includes the foreign travel emergency benefit if you plan to travel internationally.

Costs
- Determine your maximum Medicare exposure and your ability to cover those costs—that is, your monthly Medigap premium plus the costs not covered by the Medigap policy. For many beneficiaries, one cost is the Part B deductible.

- Calculate your drug out-of-pocket costs with the Medicare Plan Finder at www.medicare-links.com/medicare-plan-finder.

Coverage Rules
- If you will have a surgery that could be considered cosmetic in nature or you need power mobility devices, check into the prior authorization rules.
- Otherwise, there is no homework on coverage rules. For medically necessary care, there are no prior authorization requirements. You can choose doctors who will see Medicare beneficiaries and don't need referrals.

Extra Benefits
- Check out stand-alone dental and vision plans. The Original Medicare Path does not cover routine dental and vision care.
- Build coverage into your budget for a hearing aid.
- Investigate options to pay for LTC. (See chap. 8, "Long-Term Care [LTC].")

Medicare Advantage Path
If you are leaning toward Medicare Advantage, here are a few things you need to do.

Physicians
- Check the online directory, and contact your physicians' billing offices to investigate your physicians' participation in networks.
- Determine your willingness to find new physicians, knowing that networks can change.

Travel
- Consider a PPO plan for travel in the United States. Then check the plan's information for details about how the coverage works and your costs. Plans can have

extended networks or identify certain cities or counties that are considered in-network.

- Investigate a plan's coverage of foreign travel if that is in your future. Some do offer it.

Coverage Rules

- Read the rules and know your responsibilities for obtaining prior authorization. Given that 99 percent of Medicare Advantage plan members are in plans requiring authorization, you'll probably have to deal with this.
- Realize that, if choosing an HMO plan, you likely will need referrals to see other physicians.

Costs

- Identify a plan's out-of-pocket maximum limits. Sometimes plans with higher premiums offer lower limits.
- Calculate your maximum Medicare exposure and your ability to cover those costs.
- Determine your drug costs with the Medicare Plan Finder at www.medicare-links.com/medicare-plan-finder.

Extra Benefits

- Identify the benefits you need or would like to have.
- Check the plan's information for limits and requirements.

Factors to Consider

Finally, before you confirm your path choice, think about these factors.

Your Health

- This is significant because of costs, decisions about care, and future underwriting concerns.
- If you're healthy now, know that things can change at any time. Are you concerned about any family history?

Your Risk Tolerance
- The Original Medicare Path is for a budgeter. Pay premiums, and you have an idea of your costs.
- Medicare Advantage offers considerably lower premiums but can come with a risk of higher out-of-pocket costs.

Your Ability to Change Paths
- Study the information in chapter 3, "Changing Paths down the Road." Getting a Medigap policy in the future depends on whether you have a guaranteed issue right.
- On the other hand, Medicare Advantage plans cannot deny any eligible applicant, no matter your health status.

Medicare Advantage Commercials

If you watch any television, you've probably seen the commercials for Medicare Advantage plans. These ads feature football MVPs and television celebrities, as well as normal people.

All the commercials, no matter the narrator, talk about the Medicare benefits you deserve, that you should be getting. They list those benefits in a very big and bold font and encourage you to call the toll-free number and sign up today.

For the ones I watched, everything that these commercials report about the costs and benefits is true, to the extent that it is said. But the important information that is left unsaid is what you need to make a smart decision.

Here are some of the claims the commercials make.

Get the benefits you deserve, including rides to medical appointments, private home aides, and meals after hospitalization.
These are benefits for daily maintenance, and Medicare doesn't cover them. Because of policy changes,

Medicare Advantage plans can now offer them. However, the commercials don't provide information about these benefits.

- These are common in HMO plans, generally only available through a network of selected providers, which can limit the individual's choice.
- The plan can require prior authorization.
- There are limits on these benefits. For instance, an individual could receive two meals a day for five days after hospitalization with a limit of four hospitalizations and a private home aide up to four hours a day for no more than 31 days in a year.
- There may also be a limit on the number of benefits you can choose.

Free preventive services.

The commercials list some popular preventive services. However, Medicare now covers a long list of preventive and screening services. You don't need to enroll in a Medicare Advantage plan to get these services. (See chap. 6, "Part B, Medical Insurance.")

No premium, deductible, or copayments.

It is very possible to get a Medicare Advantage plan with no premium or deductible. However, copayments are a different story. You will find plans that do not have a copayment for the primary physician, but it's likely that other services will have out-of-pocket costs. Plan members will pay their share of costs until they reach the plan's out-of-pocket maximum limit.

See if you qualify for $144 a month; or, *Get up to $1,700 back next year.*

Definitely, the most tempting claim is the Medicare giveback benefit, officially the Part B premium reduction. Even though this has been around since

2003, it's been a big deal recently, and it's likely having an impact on many beneficiaries' decisions. Here are a few details about this giveback.

- You won't get the money back in your pocket. Rather, there is a reduction in the Part B premium you must pay.
- You qualify for this benefit if you enroll in a plan that offers it. Unfortunately, you may not find one. Last year, I checked Advantage plans in one zip code in each of three cities—Fort Lauderdale, Chicago, and Los Angeles. Just 23 percent of the plans offered premium reductions. Each plan determined the amount.
- A $144 giveback is rare. The givebacks in the three zip codes ranged from $20 to $140. Only two plans—both were Florida HMOs, and one didn't include drug coverage—offered the maximum, $144.

If you're interested in these benefits, do not call the number on the screen. The fine print says something like, "You'll be transferred to an agent who may or may not sell plans in your area that may or may not have the benefits you want." Instead, do your homework, find a plan, then talk with a licensed agent or a plan representative.

Questions and Answers Your Medicare Path Decision

How does the maximum out-of-pocket limit affect my Medicare path decision?

You need to determine your comfort level with a plan's limit.

The commercials say that Medicare Advantage plans cap your costs, which protects you from having to pay an unlimited amount for your health care. That's because these plans must establish a maximum out-of-pocket limit on the cost sharing that plan members face. Plans can have no or very low premiums, but plan members write checks for deductibles, copayments, or coinsurance for covered services. (Each plan determines its cost sharing.) These costs count toward the limit. Once the limit is reached, the plan covers any costs for the remainder of the year. The limit resets come January, and plans can change it each year.

Is it true that Original Medicare has no cap, so I could face unlimited costs?

TV commercials will tell you that Original Medicare has no limit on the costs you can face, and that is true. Part A, hospital insurance, and Part B, medical insurance, by themselves have no cap. The Part B 20 percent coinsurance for every radiation or chemotherapy treatment alone could bankrupt a person diagnosed with cancer.

However, that can change if you opt for the Original Medicare Path with a Medigap policy. You pick a package of benefits and pay the premium. Then you know the out-of-pocket costs you'll face. Pay your premiums for Plan G, see participating doctors, and the most you will pay in bills would be the Part B deductible. Basically, once you pay that, you've reached the maximum limit.

Is a Medicare Advantage plan cheaper than Original Medicare?

This question certainly reflects what we read and hear. Here are just two samples that you might find when doing a web search about Medicare costs.

> Medicare Advantage plans can cost you less than Original Medicare.

> These individuals have Original Medicare, not the cheaper Medicare Advantage plans.

As written, these claims are correct. Medicare Advantage can be cheaper than Original Medicare, which is just Part A and Part B. Unlike Medicare Advantage plans, these two parts have no limit or cap on how much you might spend.

But if we compare Medicare Advantage to the Original Medicare Path, the equation can change. Add a Medigap policy to Part A and Part B, and your costs would be the monthly premiums plus the Medigap plan's cost sharing. As previously mentioned, the most you would pay in out-of-pocket costs with Plan G is the Part B deductible.

Don't Rush Your Medicare Advantage Decision

Medicare is complex, and making a decision about your coverage takes time and study, something that many do not want to do. They want to take the quick and easy path. Then one day, they discover how the coverage works, and they don't want it anymore. Whether their situation is "fixable" depends on so many pieces.

During the OEP, we hear from Medicare Advantage members who tell us that things have not worked out as they had planned or it's costing them too much. In just about every case, we discover they chose the plan with the lowest premiums, the benefits they deserve, or the one that added money back to their Social Security checks. They didn't know about networks, prior authorization, or out-of-pocket maximums. They never realized that fixing things could be difficult, maybe even impossible.

Drift back to your high school or college days, and think about the most difficult assignment, the one that had a big impact on your final grade. You were no doubt stressed, anxious, wondering how you would do this.

If you started when it was assigned, you were able to focus, consider all the angles, revise and correct, and do a great job by the deadline. However, if you cut corners or waited until the night before it was due, you were likely stressed and didn't get the grade you wanted.

As an educator, I encourage you to be a good student and think of Medicare as the most difficult, confusing class you ever took. Give yourself time. Turn off the TV, and study your options. Compare the two paths. Think about how the coverage will work—not only today but in the future—as your health and circumstances change. You may have this coverage for a long time, so make a careful and informed decision.

Medicare Advantage offers many benefits, but you need to know what you're getting into and your opportunities to make changes. Otherwise, you may discover that haste makes waste, and there's no turning back.

It is very important to go beyond the monthly premiums to the total costs you could face in a year. That would be the premiums plus the out-of-pocket costs for the Original Medicare Path and the low premiums plus the out-of-pocket maximum for the Medicare Advantage Path. It is very possible that the Original Medicare Path could be a better deal, particularly for someone with medical issues. (See chap. 3, "Making Your Path Medicare Decision.")

Know When You Need More Help

I am often asked why Medicare has gotten so difficult. One reason is that our lives have become more complicated. When Medicare took effect in 1965, the first beneficiaries had already lived longer than the experts thought. (Life expectancy for those born in 1900 was 47 years.) They qualified for full Social Security benefits at age 65, and with Medicare, they had health care in retirement. There was just Part A and Part B, and it worked the same for everyone.

But then, as life expectancies increased, people started working longer and delayed retirement and Medicare enrollment. Retiree plans, COBRA continuation coverage, Medigap policies, and managed Medicare, now Medicare Advantage, along with advances in medical care, all have had an impact on Medicare. From Part A and Part B with the same premium for everyone, Medicare has become a complex and complicated system.

It's time to look at some situations that, if not handled correctly, can result in delayed coverage, missed opportunities, extra costs, and penalties.

Coverage after Age 65 Not Related to Current Employment

After retirement, many have the option of retiree plans or COBRA continuation plans. This coverage can cause two problems if you're not paying attention.

1. *You can miss your chance to enroll in Part B.*
   Chapter 2, "The Part B Special Enrollment Period (SEP)," addressed the opportunity for those who retire after age 65 to enroll without penalty or delay. However, too many don't realize they need to enroll and miss their chance. Then they cannot enroll until the General Enrollment Period (GEP) and can face a late enrollment penalty. Here's an example.

   Scott retired at age 65; he enrolled in Part A, hospital insurance; and he and his wife signed up for his company's retiree plan. Two years later, when his wife turned 65, she enrolled in Medicare, and he decided it was time to add Part B, medical insurance. He was shocked to discover he could not enroll until January, and he would face a late enrollment penalty. (See chap. 2, "The General Enrollment Period [GEP].")

Scott's retiree plan was sponsored by his employer. It looked and felt the same as the EGHP but with one big difference. It was not related to his current employment; he had retired. He didn't qualify for a Part B SEP and had to wait until the GEP to enroll in Part B.

2. *There is no primary payer.*
   By law, any coverage after age 65 that is not based on current and active employment becomes the secondary payer to Medicare. (The one exception is FEHB plans; however, that coverage also can have issues.) Health care providers submit the claim to Medicare first, and then they submit whatever costs Medicare doesn't cover to the retiree, individual, or COBRA plan.

   Lucia, age 68, lost her job during the COVID pandemic. She signed up for Part A and COBRA continuation coverage. Ten months later, she broke her ankle. She was stunned when she got bills for the emergency services and follow-up care.

   Lucia was eligible for Part B and should have enrolled during her SEP. Because this was the same coverage she had for years, she didn't think she needed Part B. However, Medicare, and not the COBRA plan, was the primary payer. Without a primary, there is no secondary payer, and it's like not having any coverage at all.

What Should You Do?
No matter the coverage you may have after age 65, enroll in Medicare Part B when your employment is ending.
   After age 65, if you won't have an EGHP, either through your job or through that of your spouse, enroll in Part B shortly

before or after your employment ends. The Part B SEP provides an eight-month window for enrollment. However, it's best to do this as soon as possible to avoid any gaps in coverage.

Retiree Plans
Your Ability to Change Coverage
Depends on the Plan Sponsor
Many retirees have the option to enroll in coverage sponsored by their former employer or union. The retiree plan may offer discounted premiums or cost sharing and benefits not available to the public. In many cases, the retirees have earned this coverage, may be vested, or have a fund of money, possibly from unused sick days, to apply toward the costs.

As discussed in the previous points, retirees must enroll in Part A and Part B either during their IEP or during their SEP. Medicare will be the first, or primary, payer. As the first payer, Medicare is responsible for all or most of the health care bills, even if it is not always the first one to pay. Then the retiree plan will step in to pay its share of the cost for covered services. How the retiree group health plan coverage coordinates with Medicare depends on the terms of the specific plan.

With retiree coverage, the plan sponsor controls the coverage and can change the structure, costs, or whatever else. If that happens, the retiree's options to change coverage depend on the situation.

1. *The group retirement coverage no longer works for the retiree.*
   Perhaps the premiums have increased significantly, the plan has networks with a limited ability to choose physicians, or there are significant customer service issues. Here's what happened several years ago.

   Retired teachers in a midwestern state had a plan everyone loved—with their choice of physicians, coverage when they traveled, and no bills after meeting the deductible. Then one year, everything changed. All retirees were enrolled in a special Medicare Advantage plan, and many were not happy about that.

Unhappy retirees could opt out of the coverage and choose a Medicare option available to the public, either a Medicare Advantage plan or a Medigap policy (Medicare supplement plan) and Part D drug plan. However, those who had been enrolled in Part B for more than six months no longer had a guaranteed issue right to get a Medigap policy.

2. *The sponsoring company decides to discontinue the group retirement coverage.*
In this case, the retirees lose coverage through no fault of their own and have the opportunity to elect the Medicare path of their choice. They could choose Original Medicare with a Part D drug plan and have a guaranteed issue right to get a Medigap policy. Or they could elect a Medicare Advantage plan with prescription drug coverage.

What Should You Do?
Evaluate your retiree options.

Retiree coverage may be a lifelong option. Recognize that the plan can change at any time. If you quit the retiree plan, you may not have a guaranteed issue right. If the plan quits on you, you get a do-over.

If the plan makes changes, take action as soon as you receive a notification from the company.

Get the details, and don't miss any deadlines.

Part A and Part B Only
Why Pay for Extra Coverage You Don't Need?

Almost 20 percent of those enrolled in Part A and Part B do not have any additional coverage, such as a Medigap policy, a

Medicare Advantage plan, retiree coverage, or the like. These individuals may be saving money on premiums, but they face huge medical bills if they get sick, such as in this situation.

> At retirement, Percy enrolled in Part A and Part B only. He was healthy, could afford the occasional medical bills, and didn't see the need to pay for additional coverage. Then he injured his leg with a chainsaw. He developed an infection, which led to an amputation. He had to pay the hospital deductible, the SNF copayment for 10 days, and 20 percent coinsurance for all outpatient services.

With only Part A and Part B and no additional coverage, there is no limit on the costs Percy faces. He can fix that during one of the OEPs. It's unlikely he'll get a Medigap policy unless he lives in one of the four states with continuous open enrollment. (See chap. 3, "Changing Paths down the Road.") He could get a Medicare Advantage plan because there is no medical underwriting.

What Should You Do?
Don't delay an important decision.

When enrolling in Part A and Part B, investigate additional coverage while all options are available. Don't leave yourself vulnerable to unlimited out-of-pocket costs. (See chap. 3, "The Two Medicare Paths.")

Domestic Partners
Not Being Married Can Create Medicare Problems

Domestic partners, whether of the same or opposite sex, live together as a couple but are not formally married. They frequently can qualify for spousal benefits, like health coverage through the partner's EGHP. Naturally, many think this will work the same way once they turn 65. Unfortunately, a domestic partner is not a spouse for Medicare purposes because there is no legal marriage.

Here's what happens: In a marriage, spouses can delay Part B enrollment until the working spouse retires. Then they can qualify for a Part B SEP. Because there is no marriage, domestic partners do not have that same right. They must qualify for their own SEP, which means they must be working and have EGHP coverage. Here's what can happen.

> When Bruce turned 65, he had coverage through his domestic partner's employment and didn't deal with Medicare. When his partner retired a year later, he discovered his mistake. He faced a delay in coverage and a late enrollment penalty for Part B.

What Should You Do?
Enroll in Medicare Part A and Part B at age 65.
A domestic partnership can provide health insurance benefits up to age 65. Then after that, Medicare rules take over. Even if you are continuing with the partner's EGHP, you should enroll in Medicare during the IEP.

Protect your guaranteed issue right.
Depending on the state of residence and type of employer plan (sponsored by a company with 20 or more employees), you can lose the guaranteed issue right to a Medigap policy after six months with Part B. (See chap. 3, "Changing Paths down the Road.") If that's a concern, you may opt for Medicare coverage and drop the group plan.

Consider marriage.
Spouses (of the same or opposite sex) who have been married at least one year before applying for Medicare can qualify for a Part B SEP, which could allow them to delay enrollment in Part B at age 65.

Investigate the status of your relationship.
A few states recognize a common-law marriage as a legal marriage so spousal privileges apply regarding Medicare.

Federal Employees Health Benefits (FEHB) Plans
The Decision: Part B or No Part B?

Federal employees, their spouses, and their children under the age of 26 are eligible to enroll in FEHB coverage. Whether working or retired, the same plans are available.

This coverage will continue to be the primary payer after their employment ends. Those with FEHB plans don't have to enroll in Medicare. The plan cannot force them to enroll, and it will continue to pay. But they still need to evaluate their Medicare enrollment options.

The decision to enroll in Part A is almost a no-brainer. There is no monthly premium for those who have paid Medicare taxes at least 10 years or have a spouse who did. And if they want to collect Social Security retirement benefits, they must enroll in Part A.

The Part B decision is more difficult. They would have to pay the standard Part B premium, which was $170.10 a month in 2022. Higher-income beneficiaries pay more. So why spend the money?

What Should You Do?
Do a cost-benefit analysis about Part B enrollment.

Part B can add benefits that the FEHB plan doesn't cover. It can expand the choice of providers to those who accept Medicare assignment. Some plans will waive the cost sharing or ease limits with Part B enrollment.

> Levar had an FEHB network-based plan. He was diagnosed with kidney failure. The nearest in-network dialysis center was 50 miles from his home. Enrolling in Part B would have given him a greater choice of facilities.

Lawrence's plan charged copayments for his physical therapy after knee surgery. The plan would have waived those costs if he had Part B.

Look at your personal situation, check the FEHB plan's details for information about how it coordinates with Medicare, and determine whether Part B is worth the additional premiums.

Know about possible repercussions.

If you put off enrolling in Part B when first eligible and miss your chance to enroll, the next opportunity is during the GEP, January 1–March 31. (See chap. 2, "The General Enrollment Period [GEP].") Plus, there can be a late enrollment penalty. (See chap. 2, "Identify Your Situation.")

Veterans
Medicare May Be Beneficial
Veterans may think they don't need Medicare because they have access to Veterans Affairs (VA) health care. However, that may not be their best option.

- Veterans must receive services at VA facilities. As aging issues set in, it may be more difficult to get to the facilities.
- The VA bases access to medical care on priority groups. Veterans with service-connected disabilities get the highest priority. Those with higher incomes and no service-connected disabilities are enrolled in the lowest groups and could have difficulty getting the necessary care.

What Should You Do?
Consider Medicare Part A and Part B enrollment.

Even though VA facilities cannot bill Medicare Part A or Part B, veterans should consider enrolling when first eligible.

- Part A enrollment is premium-free and would offer options for coverage of hospitalization and other services outside of VA facilities. Part A is also a condition of receiving Social Security retirement benefits.
- Part B enrollment would provide access to a wide range of outpatient services and facilities, particularly beneficial if the nearest VA facility is far away.

Enrolling when first eligible would also avoid the Part B late enrollment penalty. (See chap. 2, "Questions and Answers about the IEP.")

Consider Part D enrollment.

VA drug coverage is considered creditable, so veterans do not need to enroll in a Part D drug plan. However, with Medicare drug coverage, non-VA physicians would be able to prescribe medications, which could be filled at retail pharmacies wherever a veteran might be.

Evaluate additional Medicare coverage.

If you are a veteran and choose to enroll in Part A and Part B, consider additional coverage. Both a Medigap policy and a Medicare Advantage plan can improve your options for medical care if you don't live near a VA facility, you are in a lower priority group, or you want the flexibility to choose doctors and hospitals.

Even though the VA cannot bill Part A or Part B, it must bill a Medigap policy. That can help veterans in the lower priority groups with cost sharing.

Social Security Disability Insurance (SSDI)
Figure Out How to Deal with Two IEPs

Generally, those receiving SSDI payments will be enrolled automatically in Part A and Part B as of the first day of the 25th month of receiving benefit payments. Those who have amyotrophic lateral sclerosis, or Lou Gehrig's disease, will qualify for Medicare with the first payment.

These new Medicare beneficiaries will have their first IEP beginning three months before and ending three months after the month in which Medicare is effective. There are two important decisions they must make.

1. *Should they keep Part B, medical insurance?*

   They must keep Part A because that is a condition of receiving disability benefits.

   However, whether they must keep Part B depends on the coverage they have. They should contact Social Security or a disability counselor to discuss the situation and make decisions.

   If they do not need Part B, they should take action to decline it before the effective date. (See chap. 2, "Questions and Answers about the IEP.")

2. *Could Medicare be a better option?*

   For those who have to keep Part B, the IEP gives them an opportunity to evaluate their options. Medicare Advantage and Part D drug plans, the same ones for those age 65 and older, are available in all states.

   However, there is no federal requirement governing Medigap policies. Some states require Medicare supplement insurers selling plans in their states to offer them to the under-65 population. These plans can cost considerably more because SSDI beneficiaries can have complex medical situations.

The second IEP happens when the SSDI Medicare beneficiaries are approaching age 65. It's as though they never had Medicare before. They need to identify their situation and the necessary actions. (See chap. 2, "Identify Your Situation.")

What Should You Do?
Know about your two IEPs.

Take time to study your options and make appropriate Medicare decisions.

Expatriates
Where Do You Start with Medicare Enrollment?
Medicare for expatriates is like a game of 20 questions. Here's a sample.

- Do they have the 40 credits to qualify for premium-free Medicare Part A?
- Can they delay Part B enrollment?
- Will they have to pay any late enrollment penalties?
- If they are moving back to the States, when and how should they enroll?

What Should You Do?
Get answers before age 65.

Even if moving back to the United States is not in the plan, it's important to identify specifics related to your situation and get an idea of what to do. Consult with Social Security or a knowledgeable professional.

Need Help Paying Premiums?
Help Is Available
There are four Medicare Savings Programs to help lower-income beneficiaries with Medicare costs.

- Qualified Medicare Beneficiary,
- Specified Low-Income Medicare Beneficiary,
- Qualifying Individual, and
- Qualified Disabled and Working Individuals.

Each program has its own qualifications and provides different assistance.

Medicare also offers help with prescription drug costs. You must meet specific income criteria to qualify.

What Should You Do?
Investigate ways to get help.

- Find information about Medicare Savings Programs at www.medicare-links.com/medicare-savings-program.
- Find information about help with drug costs at www.medicare-links.com/help-with-drug-costs.

Questions and Answers about When You Need More Help

How come this chapter does not address TRICARE for Life (TFL)?

To qualify for TFL, eligible individuals must enroll in Part A and Part B. Once that is done, TFL coverage is automatic—no need to enroll. A Part D prescription drug plan is not necessary because TFL provides creditable drug coverage.

TFL operates very much like a Medigap policy, working with Part A and Part B. There are three options for physicians with a few differences. (See chapter 6, "Part B, Medical Insurance," for more about physicians and Medicare.)

- Participating physicians: There are no copayments because TFL covers all costs.
- Nonparticipating physicians: These doctors can add on a surcharge of up to 15 percent, which TFL will cover.
- Opted-out physicians: With just Original Medicare, a beneficiary would have to pay all the costs. However, TFL will pay 20 percent of the charges, and the beneficiary is responsible for the remaining 80 percent.

There are no enrollment fees or monthly premiums for TFL retirees. But the standard Part B monthly premium and higher-income beneficiary adjustments do apply.

What happens if a veteran needs medical care while on vacation?

Veterans who need emergency care can go to either a VA facility or a Medicare hospital.

For routine or nonemergency care, the VA facility would be the better option; however, VA prioritization requirements would apply. Veterans who are enrolled in Part A and Part B could also go to a Medicare-certified hospital or clinic. They would be subject to the out-of-pocket costs, such as the Part B deductible ($233 in 2022).

The next chapter will provide instructions for enrolling in Medicare when the time is right.

Chapter 4

Enrolling in Medicare

Many approaching age 65 believe that the first step in the Medicare process is enrolling in Part A, hospital insurance, and Part B, medical insurance. However, here we are, almost 100 pages into this book, and you still haven't learned how to enroll. That is because there are many steps you have to take first.

1. Establish a *my* Social Security account.
2. Determine your timing—that is, when you need to enroll in Medicare.
3. Figure out what to do with your existing coverage.
4. Identify whether you will enroll in Part A only or both Part A and Part B.
5. If you have no other options, pick your path: either Original Medicare (with a Medigap policy and Part D drug plan) or a Medicare Advantage plan with prescription drug coverage.

If you have mastered those, then we can tackle enrolling in Medicare.

You would think that no matter your situation, the enrollment instructions would be the same. But if I have learned one thing about Medicare, it's that nothing is like you think it should be. So just as with the discussion on timing, find your specific situation, and then follow those instructions.

There are three different timing scenarios.

1. The first instructions are for those turning 65 and en-rolling during their *Initial Enrollment Period (IEP)*.
2. The next apply to those who delayed enrollment past age 65, qualify for a *Part B Special Enrollment Period (SEP)*, and are now ready for Medicare.
3. The last scenario addresses those who missed their IEP or don't qualify for an SEP and must enroll during the *General Enrollment Period (GEP)*.

Turning 65: Enrolling in Medicare

As you learned in chapter 2, the IEP is a seven-month period surrounding a person's 65th birthday. No matter the individual circumstances, everyone must take some time during their IEP to determine what Medicare actions are necessary.

You should enroll in Medicare Part A and Part B if you fall into one of these groups.

- You will continue with a small employer group health plan (EGHP) after turning 65. By law, this is secondary to Medicare, and you need Part A and Part B to have complete coverage.
- You will not have coverage after age 65, either because you don't have any now or because you are giving it up or losing it once you turn 65.
- You have coverage that will be secondary to Medicare once you turn 65, including retiree, VA, COBRA, or indi-vidual plans.
- You have a Federal Employee Health Benefits (FEHB) plan and decided that Medicare enrollment would be beneficial.

There are three situations in which you can choose to en-roll in Part A only.

- You plan to continue working past age 65 for a company that has 20 or more employees and you do not contribute to a Health Savings Account (HSA).
- Your spouse is working for a company that has 20 or more employees and you will continue with that coverage past age 65.
- You have an FEHB plan and want to enroll in Part A only.

Social Security Retirement Benefits

When applying for Medicare, you need to know your plan for Social Security retirement benefits. That's because the application asks whether you are applying for Medicare only or Medicare and retirement benefits.

Many applicants don't know what to do about the Social Security decision. I am not a Social Security expert, but I have learned several important points worth sharing about when to apply for benefits.

Medicare and Social Security are two separate decisions.

- You can start receiving Social Security benefits at age 62. However, most people will not be eligible for Medicare until age 65.
- If you are receiving retirement benefits prior to age 65, you will be enrolled automatically in Medicare. (See chap. 2, "Identify Your Situation.") Then you must decide, before the effective date for coverage (noted on your Medicare card), whether you need Part B.
- However, if you have not yet applied for retirement benefits, you must determine whether you should enroll in Medicare. If so, then you can opt to enroll only in Medicare and delay Social Security or enroll in both.
- If you delay Medicare but apply for Social Security, you will be enrolled automatically in Part A at a minimum.

The Medicare eligibility age is 65, but Social Security's full retirement age (FRA) depends on the year you were born.

Also called the normal retirement age, this is the age when you qualify for 100 percent of the Social Security benefits calculated from your lifetime earnings history. The FRA was 65 for many years. But people are living longer and generally healthier in older age, so in 1983, Congress passed a law to raise the age gradually.

- Those born between 1943 and 1956 have reached the FRA.
- For those born in 1957, it is 66 years and six months.
- It will increase by two months every year until it hits 67 years for those born in 1960 and later.

Claiming benefits before the FRA will lower your monthly benefit payments; the earlier you file, the lower the benefits will be.

For every month after the FRA that you delay filing for benefits, your total benefit can increase by up to 8 percent a year, even if you are no longer working.

Deciding when to enroll in Social Security is very important. Consult with a financial advisor who can help with your unique situation.

Online Enrollment

Social Security has said that the most efficient way to enroll is online. You can use this online system if you are not receiving Social Security benefits. That's because you will be enrolled automatically, so you don't need to do so yourself. (See chap. 2, "Identify Your Situation.")

You will need a *my* Social Security account to do this. If you don't have one when you start the Medicare application process, you'll get a few pages in and then be directed to set up an account. You won't be able to finish the application until your account is ready to go.

Here are some important instructions for online Medicare enrollment during your IEP.

1. *Enroll in the first month or two of your IEP if you need Medicare to begin on the first day of your birth month.*
   - This will give enough time for Social Security to process your application and for you to find additional coverage.
   - If you enroll in the last four months, the effective date for Part B will be after your birth month, but you won't face any late enrollment penalties.
   - Remember, Medicare treats a birthday on the first day of the month as a birthday on the last day of the previous month. Everything shifts one month forward, so your IEP has four months before and two months after your birth month.
2. *Gather the information you will need.*
   - Find a list at www.medicare-links.com/online -enrollment-checklist.
   - Pay attention to the column for Medicare enrollment.
3. *Enroll at www.medicare-links.com/social-security -application.*
4. *Write down or print the page with the reentry number when it appears.*
   If you need a break or time to find information, use this number to reenter and complete your application.
5. *Answer the questions.*
   - Click the links for more information, and read that carefully. Most questions ask about you; however, some can be challenging.
   - Know that "group health plan" in this context refers to an employer plan. For instance, an individual or retiree plan is not considered to be a group plan.
   - Whether you are enrolling in Part A and Part B or Part A only, there is only one question that has a

different answer: "Do you want to enroll in Part B?" Answer "Yes" if you need Part B and "No" if you are enrolling only in Part A.

6. *Enter any dates to the best of your ability.*
7. *Check the box asking whether you agree to the requirements for an electronic signature.*
8. *Enter any relevant information in the "Remarks" box.*
9. *Review and edit the information.*
   Once you hit the "Submit Now" button, you cannot make any changes.
10. *Submit the information, and write down the confirmation number.*
    You may need this number to check the status of your application or communicate with Social Security if you have questions.
11. *Watch the mail for a Welcome to Medicare packet.*
    - It will include the Medicare & You handbook and your Medicare card.
    - Check that the information on the card is correct.

Over 65: Enrolling in Medicare

If you did not enroll in Medicare at age 65, there are two more opportunities.

Enroll during Your Part B SEP

According to the Bureau of Labor Statistics, there were almost 11 million people over the age of 65 still in the workforce in 2020. Some probably enrolled in Part A, hospital insurance, at age 65 and others didn't enroll in Medicare at all. They and/or their spouses can now qualify for an SEP to enroll in Medicare.

The Part B SEP is an eight-month period that begins the month after the last day of coverage or employment, *whichever comes first*. You can enroll in Medicare at any time if you still have an EGHP and the policy owner (you or your spouse) is still working. Or you can wait until the plan or employment ends and the eight-month window opens.

You must meet certain conditions to qualify for an SEP.

- At age 65, you have an EGHP based on your current employment or that of a spouse.
- After age 65, there are no gaps of eight months or longer in employment or coverage.

When you have an SEP, you will be able to determine your date for Medicare and add additional medical and drug coverage. Plus, there will be no late enrollment penalties.

There are two different enrollment scenarios.

1. *You are already enrolled in Part A and now need Part B, hospital insurance.*
   - You will need to submit two forms to your local Social Security office:
     ◦ the Application for Enrollment in Medicare Part B (Medical Insurance) (CMS-40B), and
     ◦ the Request for Employment Information (CMS-L564).
   - You will receive an updated Medicare card, with a Part B effective date.
2. *You did not enroll in any part of Medicare at age 65.*
   - You can enroll in Part A and Part B online through your *my* Social Security account. (See chap. 4, "Turning 65: Enrolling in Medicare.")
   - Social Security will contact you about submitting the Request for Employment Information (CMS-L564).
   - Watch the mail for your Welcome to Medicare packet and Medicare card.

Here's a look at the two forms you may need.

1. *The Application for Enrollment in Medicare Part B (Medical Insurance) (CMS-40B)*
   - Use this form if you are already enrolled in Part A.
   - Download it at www.medicare-links.com/enrollment -in-medicare-part-b-application.
   - In "Remarks," note the date you want Part B to take effect. If you don't, it will likely start on the first day of the next month, which may not fit into your retirement plans.

I chuckle every time I talk about CMS-40B.

It is called the Application for Enrollment in Medicare Part B (Medical Insurance). You complete this form because you are applying for Part B. The only question on the form is, "Do you want to sign up for Medicare Part B?" and the only answer is "Yes." Social Security is making sure that you really want to enroll in Part B.

---

2. *The Request for Employment Information (CMS-L564)*
   - Submit this form if you are enrolling in Part B.
   - Find it at www.medicare-links.com/request-for -employment-information.
   - Complete Section A, identifying the applicant (you) and the employee (either you or your spouse).
   - Ask a plan administrator or human resources representative at the place of employment for either you or your spouse to complete Section B.
   - When that is done, confirm that the dates of employment and coverage are accurate.

Submit the form(s) to your local Social Security office via USPS with a receipt requested, UPS, or FedEx. (Find the address at www.medicare-links.com/find-ssa-office.)

Social Security also offers the option to fax forms to (833) 914-2016. However, I have seen some issues with faxing that delayed the enrollment process.

Enroll during the GEP

The best way to describe the GEP is to say, "Sorry, you missed your chance to enroll." These are three common scenarios.

1. *Missed the IEP.*

   David's wife received her Medicare card in the mail two months before her 65th birthday. A year later, he waited for his card to arrive, but it never did, and David missed his IEP.

   His wife was already receiving Social Security retirement benefits and was enrolled automatically. He was not receiving benefits, and because he was retired, he should have enrolled during his IEP.

2. *Did not enroll during the Part B SEP.*

   Iliana retired on her 68th birthday—September 30, 2021. Her company paid for one year of COBRA continuation coverage. She was shut out when she tried to enroll in Part B in October 2022.

   Iliana's Part B SEP started on October 1, 2021, and ended on May 31, 2022, eight months after the last date of her employment. She missed her SEP, and now she must wait until the GEP in January.

3. *Does not qualify for premium-free Part A and didn't enroll during the IEP.*

   At age 65, Peter had earned only 32 retirement credits. He decided to delay Medicare enrollment until he earned the additional 8 credits. On his 67th birthday, he discovered he had to wait until the GEP to enroll.

   Because he didn't qualify for premium-free Part A, Peter should have enrolled during his IEP.

The GEP runs from January 1 to March 31 every year. Part B takes effect on the first day of the month after enrollment. If you find yourself in this situation, here are some points to know.

- *Enroll in Part A, if necessary, at any time.*
  Sometimes those who realize they must wait until the GEP for Part B may not be enrolled in Part A. If you qualify for premium-free Part A, you can enroll online at any time; you do not have to wait until January. Part A will provide coverage for hospitalization while you wait to enroll in Part B.
- *Enroll in Part B during the GEP.*
  You may want to contact Social Security to confirm the details of your situation and the necessary actions. Social Security will instruct you to complete the Application for Enrollment in Medicare Part B (Medical Insurance) (CMS-40B). You'll have the opportunity to add additional coverage: a Medigap policy and Part D drug plan or a Medicare Advantage plan.
- *Prepare to pay a late enrollment penalty.*
  Enrolling during the GEP may come with a Part B late enrollment penalty. (See chap. 2, "Questions and Answers about the IEP.") The penalty amount can change every year, and it applies for life.

Questions and Answers about Enrolling in Medicare

How can I check the status of my application?

Your confirmation number from your online Medicare application can help you check the status of your application after five business days. Go to www.ssa.gov, select "Check Your Application Status," and enter your confirmation number.

You may also contact Social Security at (800) 772-1213 to address any issues.

Do you have any tips for making this enrollment process less stressful?

Medicare enrollment can indeed be challenging. Here is my best tip to reduce stress: start as early in the process as you can.

You read in chapter 1 that you should have a *my* Social Security account before Medicare is even on the horizon. Then if you need to enroll at age 65, do it during the early days of your IEP. Or if you work past age 65, start the process two to three months before retirement.

It seems as though those who procrastinate run into some problems, which can further delay the process. Read this real-life story.

> Mary Jo's IEP started in February. She was helping with a new grandbaby, moving into a condo, and experiencing lots of life-changing events. She had seven months, so she wasn't worried. But then her grandbaby had medical issues, and Mary Jo got pneumonia. Suddenly, it was the last month of her IEP. She could not establish a *my* Social Security account. After finally getting through to Social Security, she learned her current name did not match the records. She never informed Social Security about her name change after her divorce. She was not able to resolve the problem in time, and she missed her chance to enroll. Now Mary Jo has to wait until the GEP in January.

If I will be retiring in April, should I enroll in Part B during the GEP?

Even though you may enroll sometime between January and March, you're technically doing this during your Part B SEP, not the GEP. To avoid a late enrollment penalty, you'll need to submit two forms (CMS-40B and CMS-L564), not just the one (CMS-40B).

Can you explain the retroactive Part A effective date?

There are two policies at work with this issue.

- Social Security has a Policy on Retroactivity. For those who file for retirement benefits after their FRA, Social Security can pay up to six months retroactively. If claiming the retroactive benefits, Part A would be backdated. Because claiming these benefits can permanently reduce future monthly benefits, a financial advisor should help with this decision.
- The Centers for Medicare and Medicaid Services' (CMS) policy applies to those who qualify for premium-free Part A. The coverage will take effect up to six months retroactively from the time of enrollment. For those who enroll during the last four months of their IEP, that would be the first day of their birth month. If they were born on the first of a month, Part A would be effective the month before their birth month. And, for those who enroll after age 65, coverage would go back six months.

Once enrolled in Medicare, it's time to look for coverage. In chapter 5, you'll learn how to be a smart shopper.

Chapter 5

Shopping for Coverage

Do you remember how much time you spent shopping for the last car you bought? One study says car buyers spend almost 15 hours. Now it's time to shop for the additional Medicare coverage you need. How much time do you think that will take?

There haven't been any official studies, but based on my observations over the last 10 years, you're probably thinking an hour, maybe two at the most. Many I've talked with took less time than that. They called a number from a commercial or picked the same "great plan" as a friend had.

A car may be more expensive up front, but your Medicare coverage is likely a life decision. You have options for dealing with a "lemon," but if your Medicare coverage doesn't work out, you may be stuck.

You need to adopt a car-shopper mentality. Do your research, compare features and costs, and check out the quality.

Helpful Resources

You know how complex Medicare can be. And now you must select coverage that will work for you. Where do you begin?

There are many resources available to you, but do check out these three.

1. *The Medicare Plan Finder is a resource that can help you get started.*
    - This is an online searchable tool at www.medicare
      -links.com/medicare-plan-finder.

- No matter what coverage you need, enter your drugs and pharmacies.
- If you need a Part D drug plan, the Plan Finder's results page lists plans in order of the lowest "estimated total drug plus premium cost" (how much you'd pay for premiums and medication refills for the rest of the calendar year).
- If you're searching for a Medicare Advantage plan, the results will be in the same order of the lowest estimated drug costs, but you'll also find detailed information about medical benefits, the costs, and coverage rules.
- After answering four questions (zip, age, sex, tobacco use), the Plan Finder now provides price information about specific Medigap policies. You can also get contact information (phone number and website) for plans available in the state. Unfortunately, it won't be as helpful for those in Wisconsin: there is no way to get costs for specific optional benefits.
- Find an instructional video on YouTube at www .medicare-links.com/using-the-medicare-plan -finder-video.

2. *Another resource is the Medicare SHIP (State Health Insurance Assistance Program).*
   - This free service is available to anyone who is eligible for Medicare.
   - Counselors assist beneficiaries to make informed health insurance decisions.
   - The training for counselors covers the basics of Medicare, the coordination of benefits, appeals, and other topics.
   - An important consideration is this: SHIP counselors do not sell insurance.
   - Find a counselor in your state at www.medicare -links.com/find-ship-counselor.

3. *An insurance agent can be a good resource to help you understand the specifics about plans, costs, and more.* Remember these two important points about working with an agent.
   1. Don't let the agent make decisions for you.
   2. Realize the best plan for you may not be one an agent sells.

   Do your homework so you understand the basics of the coverage and identify specifically what you need. Then meet with an agent who can provide more information. (See chap. 5, "Questions and Answers about a Medicare Advantage Plan.")

This chapter notes 2022 Medicare costs. Find annual updates at www.dianeomdahl.com/updates.

Shopping for Part D, Prescription Drug Coverage

No matter your choice of Medicare paths, you'll need drug coverage, so this section applies to you. To qualify, you must be enrolled in Part A and/or Part B. Then, if you choose the Original Medicare Path, you'll get a stand-alone Part D drug plan. If you elect the Medicare Advantage Path, you can get a plan with prescription drug coverage, known as an MA-PD plan. If not, you may be able to get a separate Part D plan. (See chap. 6, "Part D Prescription Drug Coverage.")

Questions to Evaluate Cost and Coverage

Start by answering these questions to identify factors that can have an impact on your choice.

- *How much is the monthly premium?*
  - Stand-alone plans have premiums. In 2022, the premiums started around $7 and go up to $80 or so.
  - Many Medicare Advantage plans do not charge additional premiums for drug coverage, but some plans do. The amount depends on the plan.

- *How much is the deductible?*
  - Every year, Medicare sets the standard deductible.
  - A plan can choose to charge no deductible or any amount up to the standard amount.
- *Do you take any medications subject to the deductible?*
  - You would pay the retail cost for any drugs subject to the deductible until you reach the plan's designated amount.
  - Your costs could be considerably more in the first few months of the year.
- *How much will you pay for your medications?*
  - A plan can charge a copayment—a predetermined amount, such as $5 or $45—that you would pay out-of-pocket per prescription.
  - Or the plan might charge a coinsurance, a predetermined percentage of the cost of a medication, such as 30 percent.
- *What are the tiers of your drugs?*
  - A tier is a payment classification and determines how much you'll pay.
  - Drug plans can have five or six tiers. The higher the tier, the more you'll pay.
  - Also know that the same drug can be a different tier in other plans. An oral medication, for instance, to treat diabetes can be a Tier 1, 2, or 3 drug, depending on the plan.
- *Are your pharmacies in-network?*
  - Your most cost-effective option likely will be a preferred retail pharmacy, one that has a contract with the plan to offer covered drugs at lower out-of-pocket costs than what you would pay at other pharmacies. Not every drug plan includes preferred pharmacies.
  - A standard retail pharmacy is an in-network pharmacy and offers covered drugs at the plan's negotiated price.

- ◦ Avoid an out-of-network pharmacy. It does not have a contract with the plan, and you would pay full price at this pharmacy.
- *Do you want to order your drugs by mail?*
  - ◦ Many plans offer a mail-order program that allows you to get up to a three-month supply of your covered prescription drugs sent directly to your home.

Focus on Coverage, Cost, and Quality

As you look for drug coverage, focus on these three important elements.

Coverage

- The plan should cover all your prescribed medications.
  - ◦ You can start with the Medicare Plan Finder to identify those plans.
  - ◦ On the plan comparison page, you'll see a notation about drugs that the plan covers, such as two of two drugs. If you opt for a plan that covers one of two, you would pay full price for the non-covered drug.
- Review the plan's coverage rules.
  - ◦ Most plans have quantity limits. For example, if the physician orders a drug to be taken daily, most plans will provide only 30 pills in one month.
  - ◦ Prior authorization can delay the start of a new medication. There are some drugs, however, that will require approval no matter which plan you choose.
  - ◦ Step therapy can be the most challenging. If there's a drug that is cheaper than the one the doctor ordered, you have to try that first. (See chap. 6, "Part D, Prescription Drug Coverage.")
  - ◦ If possible, try to avoid a plan with prior authorization or step therapy requirements.

Cost
- Pay attention to the total costs for the year—the monthly premiums plus your cost sharing (deductible, copayments, and coinsurance). Contrary to what you might think, the most cost-effective plan may not be the one with the lowest premium or deductible.
- Compare the costs at different pharmacies in your area, not just your favorite one. You might find a new way to save money.
- Also look for any pharmacies in locations where you spend considerable time.
- If necessary, access the plan's formulary, available online through the plan's website, to clarify or confirm costs.

Quality

The Medicare Plan Finder includes information about a plan's quality rating. At the very bottom of the plan details page, you'll find the quality indicators, more commonly called star ratings. Medicare rates drug plans on a 5-star basis, with five stars being the best. (See chap. 5, "Questions and Answers about Part D, Prescription Drug Coverage.")

According to the Centers for Medicare and Medicaid Services (CMS), 54 percent of plans in 2022 received four or more stars, and 10 percent received five stars, which represents the highest level of quality. Try to avoid two-star plans.

Enroll in the Plan

If you're shopping for a Medicare Advantage plan, you will need to learn about medical coverage before enrolling. Remember what you have learned in this chapter on choosing drug coverage, and apply that to the Medicare Advantage plans you evaluate.

Don't Focus Just on the Premium

You might want to simplify your search for a drug plan by just getting the one with the lowest premium. That may be simple, but you probably won't be happy with the costs. The Medicare Plan Finder can help you focus on the total costs you'll pay.

After entering your drugs and pharmacies, you'll find a section labeled "Lowest premium plus drug costs." For more information about what this means, click on this term on the plan comparison page, and you'll read, "Only includes the estimated costs to fill the drugs you entered at the pharmacies you chose plus your premiums for the months left in this year. Doesn't include any estimated health costs." In other words, if you are looking for a drug plan in March, the Plan Finder will predict how much you'll pay in premiums and cost sharing (your out-of-pocket costs) for the rest of the year, beginning in April. You may find that the lowest premium does not lead to the lowest costs for you.

Juanita takes one medication. She thought that the plan with the lowest premium available to her, $6.90, would be her best option. However, then she looked more closely. The plan's copayment for her drug, a Tier 2, was $19. The total cost for the year (the monthly premium plus copayments) would be $310.80.

She looked at a second plan with a premium of $9.80 and a copayment of $10 for her drug. However, her drug, a Tier 2 in this plan, was subject to the deductible. She would meet the deductible in October. Her total drug costs would be $605.60.

Finally, Juanita found a plan with a $14.60 premium. In this plan, her drug was a Tier 1 with a $4 copayment. Her annual costs would be $223.20. Paying more in premiums saved her money.

If you chose the Original Medicare Path, once you have decided on the drug plan that's right for you, it's time to enroll.

You can contact a customer service representative of your selected plan. This is the best approach if you have questions about any drug issues. During this call, you can:

- confirm the monthly premium,
- verify that the plan covers your prescribed medications and includes your pharmacies in-network,
- address any cost concerns,
- indicate the date that you want the plan to take effect,
- make payment arrangements, and
- complete the enrollment process.

You can also enroll online through the plan's website.

Remember, drug coverage is a one-year deal. Every year, plans change. In late September, watch for the Annual Notice of Changes from your plan, and then decide whether you want to keep your plan or switch. (See chap. 8, "Open Enrollment Period [OEP].")

Questions and Answers about Part D, Prescription Drug Coverage

What should I know about the star ratings for Part D coverage?

Each drug plan receives an overall quality rating (which shows the plan's performance as a whole) and summary quality ratings. These overall and summary ratings come from different indicators, which can shed light on a plan's performance and how it will work for you.

CMS identified these four indicators to describe the quality of a drug plan.

1. Drug plan customer service,
2. Member complaints and changes in the drug plan's performance,
3. Member experience with the drug plan, including members' ratings of the plan and ease of getting prescriptions filled, and
4. Drug safety and accuracy of drug pricing.

Each of these indicators has subcategories. Go beyond the overall rating and click on the specific data elements that will potentially have an impact on your plan experience. You might find one plan that received an overall quality rating of four stars. However, under member experience, the plan received one star for ease of getting prescriptions filled.

Is it best to enroll online or by phone?

Going online is a convenient and generally quick way to enroll. However, if you have questions, perhaps about coverage or a drug or service, you may want to talk with a plan representative.

Do I have to enroll in both Part A and Part B to get a Medicare drug plan?

No, both parts of Medicare are not required to purchase a Part D drug plan. And that's good, because there are times you may need drug coverage and don't want or need Part B. In one situation, you may have a high-deductible employer plan, and the drug coverage is not creditable. You can enroll in premium-free Part A and then purchase a drug plan.

Shopping for a Medicare Advantage Plan

After enrolling in Part A and Part B, you've decided that you want a Medicare Advantage plan. If you think shopping for this coverage will be easy, think again. In 2022, the average person had 39 Medicare Advantage plans available, more than double the number in 2017. In some locations, there were over 50 plans. There can be two to four or more different types of plans sponsored by 10–15 insurance companies. Every plan has different costs, benefits, and star ratings.

As you learned in chapter 3, "Making Your Medicare Path Decision," commercials pitch all the great benefits and low costs with Medicare Advantage plans. But now that you are shopping for a plan, remember these dos and don'ts.

- Don't enroll in an Advantage plan just for the extra benefits.
- Instead, do investigate the essential benefits you'll need, like coverage for specialists and physical therapy.
- Don't call the number on the screen.
- Rather, do your homework. Go beyond the commercials, and get the information you need to make a smart decision. Find the best plan, and then connect directly with that insurer or a licensed agent.

You can sense that you face a big challenge. How do you know which plan to choose? Here's a syllabus to help you get started. (If you need drug coverage, review chapter 5, "Shopping for Part D, Prescription Drug Coverage." This syllabus focuses on shopping for medical coverage.)

Determine the Type of Plan You Need

There are several types of Medicare Advantage plans, but not every type is available everywhere. Chances are you'll choose either an HMO (health maintenance organization) or a PPO (preferred provider organization), the two most popular plans.

HMO Plans
- HMOs account for almost 60 percent of the available plans.
- There are likely zero-premium plans available in just about every location.
- Members will probably need to select a primary physician who will coordinate care.
- Members must see providers in the network for routine (nonemergency) medical care.
- Other than for true emergency situations, an HMO may not pay for care outside the network.
- In most HMO plans, a referral from the primary physician is necessary to see a specialist or other health care provider.
- HMO plans can also require prior authorization.
- These plans tend to have lower cost sharing and out-of-pocket maximums than PPO plans.
- These plans can include drug coverage. However, if there is no drug coverage, members cannot purchase a stand-alone Part D plan.

Who should consider an HMO plan? Those who can live with a network, are willing to change doctors, and would like lower costs.

PPO Plans
- PPOs make up over 35 percent of available plans.
- These plans are more likely to have premiums than HMO plans.
- Members have the flexibility to choose doctors, specialists, or hospitals that aren't in the plan's network.
- Nonnetwork physicians have no obligation to treat nonmembers, except in an emergency.

- Out-of-network services can cost more—in some cases, 30–50 percent of the costs.
- PPOs can require prior authorization.
- These plans can include Part D drug coverage. However, if there is no drug coverage, members cannot purchase a Part D stand-alone plan.
- There are two types of PPOs.
  - A local PPO has a small service area, such as a county or part of a county.
  - A regional PPO has a contracted network that serves an entire region or regions. This plan must do business in regions defined by the government, including both urban and rural areas.

Who should consider a PPO plan? Those who will need coverage out-of-network, want the flexibility to choose physicians, and can afford the higher cost sharing.

There are more types of plans available; however, these are not as common.

Private Fee-for-Service (PFFS) Plans

- Seeing providers in-network will be the most cost-effective option.
- However, members can choose to see any Medicare-approved provider who will accept the plan's terms and conditions of payment. These services can cost more than in-network care.
- These plans may or may not include drug coverage. If no coverage is included, members can buy a stand-alone Part D drug plan.
- A PFFS plan cannot require prior authorization of services.
- In recent years, the number of PFFS plans has declined, and these plans now account for about 1 percent of enrollees. These plans are not available to every beneficiary.

Who should consider a PFFS plan? Those who want the freedom and are willing to pay more to see any provider who accepts Medicare assignment and still have access to any benefits the plan may offer.

Medical Savings Account (MSA) Plans

- There may or may not be a network of contracted providers.
- However, the plans cannot restrict services to a network. Members can see any physician who will accept Medicare patients.
- MSA plans cannot include drug coverage, so members must purchase a stand-alone Part D prescription drug plan.
- There are no monthly premiums.
- Some plans offer extra benefits, sometimes for an additional monthly charge.
- There are two parts to these plans.
  - A high deductible: The member must pay this before the plan contributes anything. Only Medicare-covered expenses count toward the deductible. Once it is met, the plan covers all Part A and Part B expenses. The amount of the deductible varies from plan to plan and year to year.
  - A Medical Savings Account: The member sets up an account at a bank the plan selects. Unlike a Health Savings Account (HSA), the member cannot contribute to an MSA. The plan decides how much money to contribute and deposits money into the account. In one MSA plan, the deductible is $5,400, and the plan contributes $1,500 to the savings account.
- Plan members can use funds from their savings accounts to pay for deductibles and other qualified medical expenses. The funds can carry over into the next year.

- MSA plans were available in limited areas with fewer than 6,000 enrollees in 2019.

Who should consider an MSA plan? Those who believe their health expenses won't exceed the deductible or will meet the deductible quickly and want the freedom to choose doctors who accept Medicare assignment.

Special Needs Plans (SNP)
- These plans limit membership to people with specific diseases or characteristics.
- SNPs may charge a premium.
- An SNP features focused care management, special expertise of physicians and other health care providers, and benefits tailored to meet special needs.
- These plans can require referrals and prior authorization.
- SNPs must also include prescription drug coverage.
- There are about four million SNP enrollees.

Who should consider an SNP plan? These plans are available to three groups of beneficiaries:

- dual-eligible beneficiaries (eligible for both Medicare and Medicaid),
- residents of a nursing home or other institution, and
- those with chronic conditions, including chronic alcohol and other drug dependence, cancer, chronic heart failure, dementia, diabetes mellitus, HIV/AIDS, and stroke.

Focus on Coverage, Cost, and Quality
After familiarizing yourself with the types of plans, then it's time to research three important elements.

Coverage

Figuring out how a plan will cover the services and medications you need can be more important than the costs. Get the answers to these questions.

- Are your physicians in-network?
- Does the plan have referral requirements?
- Does the plan require prior authorization?
- Are your drugs covered?
- Are your pharmacies in-network?
- Does the plan offer any additional benefits you may want, like dental, vision, transportation, fitness, or others?

Cost

Simply put, figure out how much you will pay if you choose a particular plan. Those costs include the following.

- Monthly premiums: Chances are you will find zero-premium plans.
- Health and drug plan deductibles: Many health plans do not have deductibles.
- Out-of-pocket costs for services: The plan's maximum limit is the most you could pay in a year for medical services.
- Total drug costs: Add up the drug plan premium, deductible, and the costs sharing for prescription medications.

Quality

The Medicare Part C star ratings address the quality of a Medicare Advantage plan on a 5-star scale, with five being the highest and one being the lowest. (See chap. 5, "Questions and Answers about a Medicare Advantage Plan.")

CMS reported that in 2022, 68 percent of Medicare Advantage plans that offer prescription drug coverage received four-star ratings, with 74 getting five stars.

Check Out Plans

Once you understand the basics about Medicare Advantage plans, the best place to start would be with the Plan Finder. On the plan results page, you can search for the type of plan you want—for instance, an HMO or PPO.

The details page for a plan will shed more light on costs and coverage rules (e.g., plan limits and referral or prior authorization requirements). But to avoid any future surprises, study the plan's Evidence of Coverage (EOC). This is likely the most important document that gets the least attention. To find the EOC, click on the link to the plan's website (on the details page), and then look for the plan's documents. The location will be different for every plan.

CMS provides a template, so every plan's EOC follows the same format. Review the table of contents so you know what is in the document, and pay special attention to these chapters.

- Using the plan's coverage for your medical services: topics include getting services in- and out-of-network and emergency situations.
- Medical benefits chart (what is covered and what you pay): probably the most important section, identifying costs, coverage rules, and details for benefits (listed in alphabetical order).
- What to do if you have a problem: coverage decisions, appeals, and complaints.

The next step is to check on whether your physicians and health care providers are in the plan's network. Again, this probably won't be easy to find. CMS has standards for the content of provider directories, but every insurer has a different tool. If doing this through the website is frustrating, you can call the plan or your physicians' offices. (Remember that networks can change at any time.)

Enroll in the Plan

Once you have settled on the plan you want, it's time to enroll. There are three ways to do this.

1. Call the plan. You'll find the number in the Medicare Plan Finder or on the plan's website.
2. Enroll online through either the Plan Finder or the plan's website.
3. Contact an agent.

During the enrollment process, do the following.

- Get answers to your questions about benefits or costs.
- Confirm that your physicians and health care providers are in-network and your medications are covered.
- Set up payment arrangements.

Once you're enrolled, the plan will send your member ID card and additional information about the following items:

- how to find important documents, including the EOC, drug formulary, and pharmacy and provider directories,
- billing, and
- any other plan-specific details.

Remember, you have two opportunities every year to evaluate your Medicare Advantage plan and make a change, if necessary. (See chap. 8, "Changing Plans.")

Questions and Answers about a Medicare Advantage Plan

How do I find a good agent?

If you do an internet search, you'll find many tips, but there are some common points among these results.

- Decide whether you want to work with a captive or independent agent. Captive agents sell plans from one company; independent agents offer plans from more than one.
- Get referrals or recommendations.
- Ask about credentials.
- Visit websites.
- Talk with the agent before starting the plan selection process. The agent's knowledge and your trust in him or her are the most important factors in a successful relationship.

If you have a good relationship, the agent can help you with issues or problems once you are enrolled in the plan.

What should I know about the star ratings for Medicare Advantage plans?

Besides an overall rating, Medicare Advantage plans get two sets of summary ratings, one for the health plan and the other for the drug coverage. (See more information in chapter 5, "Questions and Answers about Shopping for Part D, Prescription Drug Coverage.")

Medicare evaluates the health plan (medical coverage) in five areas.

1. Staying healthy (screenings, tests, and vaccines),
2. Managing chronic (long-term) conditions,
3. Members' experiences with the health plan, including ease of getting needed care, getting appointments and

care quickly, members' ratings of the health plan, and members' ratings of the health care quality,
4. Members' complaints and changes in the health plan's performance, and
5. The health plan customer service.

Is Medicare Advantage a supplement?

No, it is not, but I have seen several websites that refer to Medicare Advantage as supplemental coverage, which is defined as something that is provided in addition to what is already present or available to complete or enhance it. A Medigap policy enhances the coverage provided by Part A, hospital insurance, and Part B, medical insurance. Medicare.gov defines Medicare Advantage as an "all-in-one" alternative that can be chosen instead of Original Medicare.

What is a Medicare Cost Plan?

A Medicare Cost Plan provides a full package of Medicare benefits. In the Medicare Plan Finder, you'll find these plans mixed in with Medicare Advantage plans. However, Medicare Cost Plans blend parts of both Original Medicare and Medicare Advantage. These plans:

- work with Part A and Part B but provide some additional benefits and flexibility,
- have a network of doctors and hospitals with the option of out-of-network services that are covered under Medicare Part A and Part B,
- have an out-of-pocket maximum, and
- may or may not include drug coverage (if not, members can buy a stand-alone Part D drug plan).

Since 2019, the federal government has been eliminating Medicare Cost Plans from counties where two or more Medicare Advantage plans are available. As a result, most states do not have these plans. In 2019, there were about 200,000 beneficiaries enrolled in Medicare Cost Plans, and that number is likely to drop even more.

Who should consider a Medicare Cost Plan (if available)? Those who want lower costs, the flexibility to choose physicians outside the network, and the benefits a Medicare Advantage plan offers.

Shopping for a Medigap Policy

A Medigap policy, more officially called Medicare Supplement Insurance, is coverage administered by private insurance companies licensed to sell policies in a particular state. This policy helps cover the gaps in Part A, hospital insurance, and Part B, medical insurance, paying some costs—such as deductibles, copayments, and coinsurance—for Medicare-covered services that would otherwise be your responsibility.

Here are some basic points about this coverage, an essential component of the Original Medicare Path.

- To purchase a Medigap policy, you must be enrolled in both Part A and Part B.
- This is optional coverage that comes with an additional monthly premium.
- Medigap policies sold since 2006 cannot include prescription drug coverage. If you want drug coverage, you'll need to purchase a stand-alone Part D prescription drug plan.
- A Medigap policy only works with the Original Medicare Path. You cannot purchase it to help with cost sharing in Medicare Advantage plans.
- One Medigap policy covers only one person. You must have your own policy. There are Medigap insurers that offer household discounts—lower premiums when two people with the same address purchase the same policy.

- Different companies charge different premiums for the exact same coverage. As a result, once you determine the benefits you need and want in a Medigap policy, you can compare plans based solely upon the companies, agents, and prices.
- Every state has its own list of companies authorized to sell plans.

With all the companies selling different plans, how do you know what will be best for your situation? These steps may help simplify the process.

1. Understand the benefits you can get with a Medigap policy.

Medigap policies help cover the costs Original Medicare alone doesn't pay, like the inpatient hospital deductible and the Part B deductible and coinsurance. These policies can also offer optional benefits related to things that Medicare doesn't cover, like foreign travel emergency coverage.

2. Become familiar with your state's standardization of benefits.

In 47 states, plans organize benefits by letters, like Plan A or Plan G. (Massachusetts, Minnesota, and Wisconsin have their own standardization models.)

In the chart with this section, the Medigap benefits are listed down the left side. Each of these benefits connects with a Medicare cost for the calendar year. Then across the top, you'll see 10 letters. (The missing letters represent plans that are no longer sold. Beneficiaries who have those plans can keep them.) Each letter represents a different package of benefits with different cost sharing.

Plan A (not to be confused with Part A) covers only the four benefits available in every policy. Compared to other plans, it tends to be overpriced for what it covers. On the other hand, Plan F has been called the Cadillac of Medigap policies. Pay the monthly premium, and there are never any bills if you deal with providers who see Medicare patients. It pays all Part A and Part B deductibles and cost sharing. Since 2020, newly eligible beneficiaries, those who turn 65 or first become eligible for disability or end-stage renal disease (ESRD) benefits, cannot purchase Plan F or Plan C. These new beneficiaries must pay the Part B deductible. (See chap. 5, "Questions and Answers about a Medigap Policy.")

The packages of benefits for the other plans range from the basic Plan A to the Cadillac Plan F. According to AHIP, the two fastest growing plans are Plan G and Plan N.

- Plan G offers every benefit, except the Part B deductible. Pay the premium, and your maximum exposure for medical care is just the Part B deductible, which was $233 in 2022. There is also a high-deductible Plan G. After meeting the deductible, $2,490 in 2022, the plan pays benefits in full. Premiums are about 50 percent less than a regular Plan G. Some companies do not offer a high-deductible version.
- Plan N does not cover the Part B deductible and Part B excess charges. (See chap. 6, "Part B, Medical Insurance.") There can be a $20 copayment for physician visits and a $50 copayment for emergency room visits that do not result in a hospital admission. The monthly premiums are less than those for Plan G.

Know that once you pick your letter, the policy you purchase must provide the same coverage, no matter the insurance company that sells it.

Three States with Their Own Standardization Models
As mentioned, Medigap policies in Massachusetts, Minnesota, and Wisconsin do things differently. They are not identified by letter, but they must offer the same Part A and

Part B benefits, along with foreign travel emergency, and may include additional ones.

- Massachusetts
  This state has three standardized plans.
  1. The Core Plan covers the same mandatory benefits as Plan A plus inpatient mental health stays.
  2. The Supplement 1 Plan covers all Part A and Part B benefits, except for Part B excess charges, which Massachusetts' providers cannot apply. Newly eligible beneficiaries cannot purchase this plan because it offers the Part B deductible benefit.
  3. The Supplement 1A Plan covers the same benefits as the Supplement 1 Plan but excludes the Part B deductible. This is the plan that newly eligible beneficiaries can get.

  (Learn more about these plans at www.medicare-links.com/massachusetts-medigap-policies.)

- Minnesota
  The options resemble the federally standardized plans but without the identifying letters.
  - The basic plan with optional riders is similar to Plan A.
  - The extended basic plan covers all Part A and Part B benefits and foreign travel emergency, with a $1,000 out-of-pocket limit (similar to Plan F). Newly eligible beneficiaries would get this plan without the Part B deductible coverage (similar to Plan G). There is also a high-deductible option available.
  - There are plans that offer 50 percent coverage (similar to Plan K) and 75 percent coverage (similar to Plan L).
  - The 50 percent Part A deductible coverage plan resembles Plan M.

- One similar to Plan N has $20 and $50 copayment for Part B services.

Minnesota is another state that does not allow Part B excess charges.

(See www.medicare-links.com/minnesota-medigap -policies for more information.)

- Wisconsin
Think of this state's standardization of Medigap policies as a menu in a restaurant. You order a steak, and it comes with a baked potato, your basic meal. You decide to add an à la carte salad, an option available at an extra cost. Wisconsin's policies have basic benefits, included in the premium. Then there are optional benefits, each with its own price tag.

Wisconsin Medigap policies include four additional basic benefits:
  - 40 home health visits,
  - coverage for a list of non-Medicare supplies,
  - coverage for 30 days of non-Medicare skilled nursing facility care, and
  - 175 additional days of inpatient mental health care.

An optional benefit is additional home health care, up to 365 visits per year.

(Read more about Wisconsin policies at www.medicare-links.com/wisconsin-medigap-policies.)

Depending on where you live, you might be able to get a Medicare Select plan. The premiums may be lower, but these plans generally have a network of participating providers. If you go outside the network, you may have to pay some or all the costs that Part A and Part B don't cover. These plans do not include drug coverage, so you would have to purchase a stand-alone drug plan.

2022 Original Medicare Costs and Medigap Benefits

Original Medicare Costs [1]	Benefits [2]	Medicare Supplement Insurance (Medigap) Plans								Not Available to New Enrollees [7]	
		A	B	D	G	K	L	M	N [9]	C	F
Days 61-90: $389 per day; Days 91-150: $778 per day	Part A copayment (up to an additional 365 days)	100%	100%	100%	100%	100%	100%	100%	100%	100%	100%
20% after deductible	Part B coinsurance	100%	100%	100%	100%	50%	75%	100%	100%	100%	100%
Provider cost for first 3 pints	Blood	100%	100%	100%	100%	50%	75%	100%	100%	100%	100%
Inpatient respite stay 5%	Part A hospice care coinsurance	100%	100%	100%	100%	50%	75%	100%	100%	100%	100%
Days 21-100: $194.50 per day [4]	Part A skilled nursing facility copayment			100%	100%	50%	75%	100%	100%	100%	100%
$1,556 per benefit period [3]	Part A hospital deductible		100%	100%	100%	50%	75%	50%	100%	100%	100%
$233 per year	Part B deductible									100%	100%
Not accepting assignment: up to 15% more than Medicare covers	Part B excess charges				100%						100%
Foreign travel emergency (outside of the U.S.) [5]	Up to 80% for medically necessary care			✓	✓			✓	✓	✓	✓
						Out-of-pocket limit [8]					
						$6,620	$3,310				

1. Beneficiaries are responsible for these Part A and Part B out-of-pocket costs.
2. There are Medigap benefits available to help with the Medicare costs.
3. The Part A hospital deductible covers a 60-day benefit period. Depending on timing, it is possible to pay more than one deductible in a calendar year.
4. The Part A skilled nursing facility copayments also apply per-benefit period.
5. Foreign travel emergency will cover up to 80% with a deductible of no more than $250. The emergency must happen within the first 60 days of a trip.
6. The letters represent different packages of benefits and costs.
7. Plan C and Plan F are not available to newly eligible beneficiaries after 2020.
8. A beneficiary pays 50% of costs with Plan K until reaching the out-of-pocket maximum. With Plan L, the beneficiary pays 25%. These are the only two plans that have out-of-pocket maximums.
9. With Plan N, you pay $20 for some doctors' visits and $50 for emergency room visits that do not result in a hospital admission.

Adapted from "2017 Choosing a Medigap Policy: A Guide to Health Insurance for People with Medicare"

© 2022 65 Incorporated

Find a full-size copy of this chart, along with annual cost updates, at www.dianeomdahl.com/updates.

3. Investigate pricing.

As with most everything in life, premiums for Medigap policies do increase. However, each state's insurance department or commissioner must approve rate increases.

After choosing the benefits you want and need, consider how the premiums are priced. The pricing can have an impact on not only your premiums initially but also how much and how often premiums increase. Medicare rules allow three methods.

- *Attained-age-rated.*
  - These premiums are generally some of the lowest available to new enrollees.
  - However, when you attain a new age, you'll probably get a birthday present—a premium increase. For that reason, these policies tend to become more expensive over time.
- *Issue-age-rated.*
  - The premiums for these policies are based on your age when you first buy the policy and often are more in the beginning than a comparable attained-age-rated policy.
  - Premiums can increase because of rising medical costs, inflation, and other reasons, but they do not increase automatically because of birthdays.
- *Community-rated.*
  - Sometimes called no-age-rated, these policies generally charge the same monthly premium to everyone in a certain area, regardless of age.
  - Premiums can increase because of inflation and costs but not because of birthdays. In general, Medicare.gov believes these policies tend to be the least expensive over the course of a lifetime.
  - Insurance companies that sell community-rated plans may offer discounts to new enrollees. This

can make premiums more competitive initially, but over time, the discounts can decrease and eventually disappear.

Each state mandates how the Medigap policies are priced. For instance, Connecticut and New York mandate that all plans must be community-rated. In Florida, the plans are issue-age-rated. The majority of other states allow all three pricing methods. In those states, you'll find that most plans are attained-age-rated, with possibly one or two issue-age-rated and community-rated.

4. Pick the plan that you want, price shop, and enroll.

If you are in a state that has letter plans, pick the letter that represents the benefits you need. In Massachusetts, Minnesota, or Wisconsin, pick the type of plan you want.

Then check into companies that offer that plan. You can deal with either an agent or the company.

Compare prices. The plan you select, regardless of the monthly premium, must provide the benefits that come with the letter or type of plan. Ask questions such as, How is the premium priced? What is the plan's history of premium increases?

You can enroll directly with the company or an agent. During enrollment, confirm important details, indicate the date you'd like coverage to begin, and set up a payment plan.

Be Careful When Choosing Your Medigap Policy

You must have a guaranteed issue right to get the Medigap policy you want at the best price. For most, that right ends six months after you're first enrolled in Part B. You may or may not be able to make changes to this coverage in the future.

Questions and Answers about a Medigap Policy

What should I do if my doctor says she doesn't work with the insurance company that sponsors my Medigap policy?

A doctor's acceptance of a Medigap policy is based not on the insurance company sponsoring the coverage but, rather, on whether the doctor accepts assignment. If so, the doctor cannot refuse to accept the Medigap policy.

Be sure to show the doctor your card, which should say Medicare Supplement Insurance.

How come Massachusetts, Minnesota, and Wisconsin don't use letter plans?

In July 1992, the federal government introduced Medigap policies that were standardized by letters. All new Medigap policies had to conform to this standardization of benefits.

Massachusetts, Minnesota, and Wisconsin took control of Medigap policies before the federal government did. These states received waivers and were allowed to keep their plan structures.

How come newly eligible beneficiaries cannot purchase Plan F or Plan C?

The changes are the result of the Medicare Access and CHIP Reauthorization Act (MACRA) of 2015. Congress intended to increase the amount of "skin in the game" for Medicare beneficiaries. Some legislators feared that those with these plans might use more health care services than those who must pay the Part B deductible. As a result, MACRA prohibits insurance companies from offering plans that cover the Part B deductible to newly eligible beneficiaries after 2020. That includes Plan F and Plan C in the lettered plans of 47 states and plans in Massachusetts, Minnesota, and Wisconsin that offer the Part B deductible.

Just a comment about a little skin in the game. In the context of medical care, the Part B deductible ($233 in 2022) is indeed very little skin in the game. Given that the average cost of a primary physician visit can be $150 or more, you'd meet the deductible in two visits.

If I qualify for Plan F, should I get one?

There are two reasons why you may not want to get Plan F, even if you qualify.

1. You'd likely overpay for the one benefit that Plan F offers that Plan G cannot, the Part B deductible. For one plan in South Florida, the 2022 monthly premium for one company's Plan G was $253 and $297 for Plan F. Plan F cost $44 more per month, or $528 in a year, to cover a benefit worth $233, the 2022 Part B deductible.
2. The second reason is the concern that the premiums may increase significantly in future years. That's because no younger and healthier beneficiaries can purchase Plan F.

Where can I find the star ratings for Medigap policies?

Trying to evaluate the quality of these policies is difficult because there are no quality or star ratings. Medigap policies are mostly controlled by the individual states.

You may have realized that Medicare is not like any coverage you've had before. And, because of that, Chapter 6 will address important points you need to know as you go forward in life with Medicare.

Chapter 6

Living with Medicare

You're successfully navigating the road to Medicare. You enrolled and have gotten the coverage you need. Now that you're here, however, you still have more to do. You need to learn how to live with Medicare because it's likely to be the last coverage you will ever have.

Know What Coverage You Have

When beneficiaries start talking to me about a Medicare problem, the first thing I do is ask them what type of Medicare they have. In too many cases, I get a blank stare. To clarify, I ask whether it is Original Medicare with a Medigap policy (or supplement) or a Medicare Advantage plan. Then they reach for their wallet and start digging through their cards.

The type of coverage, your Medicare path, has an impact on so many aspects of your medical care. On the next few pages, you'll find examples that will help you identify your coverage and point out things you should know.

The Cards of Medicare:
Here's How to Identify Your Coverage

Your Medicare Card

After enrolling in Medicare, you will get a red, white, and blue card that notes your Medicare number ②, officially a Medicare Beneficiary Identifier (MBI). Verify that your name ①, the part(s) of Medicare you have, and the effective date(s) ③ are correct. Protect your Medicare card. Do not let anyone else use this card or your number.

Depending on the Medicare path you chose, you can have one or two additional cards.

Every card will identify the covered individual (you) and the insurance company. On the front or back of a card, you'll likely find contact information for the plan. The cards may also include the numbers for provider and member services or the benefit website.

The Medicare Advantage Path

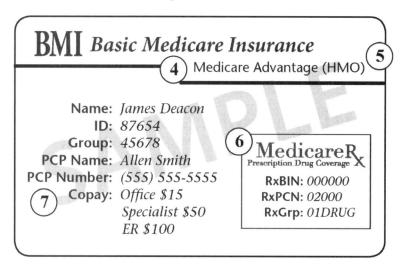

If you elected Medicare Advantage, store your Medicare card in a safe place. You will need to show only your Medicare Advantage card to doctors, health care providers, and pharmacies. Even if you don't change plans during the Open Enrollment Period, you will get a new card every year.

Every card must include "Medicare Advantage" ④ and the type of plan ⑤.

The (MedicareRx) logo ⑥ indicates that this plan includes Part D prescription drug coverage. The card also includes an RxBIN, RxPCN, and RxGroup (or Group ID). These three numbers, along with the member ID, identify the covered individual and the specific Part D coverage.

If your card does not have the MedicareRx logo and related information, your plan does not include drug coverage.

The card may also list the name and number for your primary care physician, referral required, copayments, or out-of-network charges ⑦.

The Original Medicare Path

If you chose the Original Medicare Path, you will have two cards, in addition to your Medicare card.

Medicare Supplement Insurance (Medigap Policy)

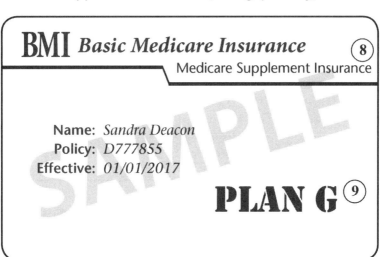

You will need to show your Medicare card, along with your Medicare Supplement Insurance card, when you receive health care services. Because the benefits for a Medigap policy do not change, you probably won't get a new card every year.

The card must note "Medicare Supplement Insurance" ⑧ and the type of plan ⑨. In 47 states, that will be a letter, identifying the package of benefits.

In Massachusetts, Minnesota, and Wisconsin, you'll find information noting the type of plan, such as a Wisconsin "Basic Plan."

Beyond that, the insurance company determines what information to put on this card.

Part D Prescription Drug Plan (PDP)

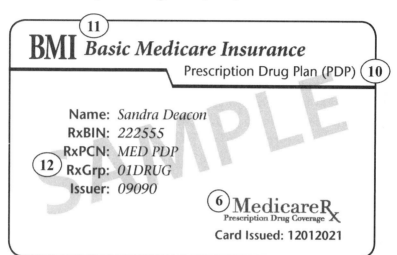

This card identifies a stand-alone Part D drug plan ⑩ and the sponsoring company ⑪. You will share it with your pharmacies.

The logo ⑥ indicates that this is Part D prescription drug coverage. The card will also include information (RxBIN, RxPCN, and RxGroup ⑫ [or Group ID]) identifying the covered individual and specific Part D coverage.

MyMedicare.gov Account

Once you have your Medicare card, you should create a MyMedicare.gov account. With this account, you can check the details of your enrollment and current Medicare coverage, check the status of claims, review health records, and more. This account will provide current information about your medications and drug coverage, so you don't have to enter all your medications every time you want to check something.

To create an account, do the following.

- Go to www.medicare-links.com/create-a-mymedicare -account.

- Enter your Medicare number, your Part A effective date, and the requested information about you.
- Create your username and password.

You may also want to set up online accounts for your other Medicare coverage, either your Medigap policy and Part D drug plan or the Medicare Advantage plan. Check your plan information or talk to a plan representative about how to do this or any concerns you have.

Coverage of Services and Medications

We were all taught that Medicare has four parts. However, as you learned in chapter 1, there are three parts that work together to meet your medical and prescription drug needs. We'll start with the three parts: Part A, hospital insurance; Part B, medical insurance; and Part D, prescription drug coverage.

There are three components to the discussion of each part of Medicare.

1. *Medicare Basics:* The rules, criteria, and maximum costs that apply, no matter the path you chose
2. *Original Medicare Path:* Important points that have an impact on beneficiaries who chose this path
3. *Medicare Advantage Path:* Significant points for those who elected this coverage

The coverage of services includes 2022 Medicare costs. Get updated information at www.dianeomdahl.com/updates.

Part A, Hospital Insurance

Medicare Part A covers four essential services.

Hospitalization
Medicare Basics
Medicare covers a hospital stay when your doctor orders an inpatient admission.

Part A coverage includes the hospital room (semiprivate, if available), nursing care, meals, drugs administered as part of the treatment plan, and other services, such as physical therapy or X-rays.

Original Medicare Path
- Medicare will pay for a stay in a hospital that accepts assignment.
- The Part A deductible for hospitalization was $1,556 in 2022. This deductible covers a 60-day benefit period.
- There is an additional per-day cost for extended hospitalizations: $389 for days 61–90, and $778 for days 91–150 (lifetime reserve days) in 2022.

(To learn more about benefit periods and lifetime reserve days, see chap. 6, "Questions and Answers about Living with Part A and Part B.")

Original Medicare and Medigap Policies Go Together

If you chose the Original Medicare Path, a Medigap policy (or a Medicare supplement plan) is a key component of this coverage. It will help cover many of the costs you'll read about in this section. For instance, every Medigap policy covers the 20 percent coinsurance for Part B services.

See chapter 5, "Shopping for a Medigap Policy," for more about how a Medigap policy works, and check your Medigap policy for complete coverage information.

Medicare Advantage Path

- Plans will cover a stay at an in-network hospital.
- A deductible may apply, and most plans charge per day, such as a $395 copayment for the first seven days.
- Some plans will cover out-of-network hospitalizations, which can cost you more. A common practice is to charge a coinsurance, such as 33 percent of the cost.
- Prior authorization rules can also apply to nonemergency admissions.

Medicare Advantage Plans Do Things Differently

In its early days, Medicare Advantage was known as a Medicare replacement plan, replacing Original Medicare. Over time, that name fell out of favor because Medicare Advantage doesn't replace Original Medicare. It is its own type of coverage that becomes Medicare for those who elect this path. However, there still seem to be some elements that resemble a replacement.

- A Medicare Advantage plan ID card replaces the red, white, and blue Medicare card.
- The titles—Part A, hospital insurance, and Part B, medical insurance—are gone, and services, such as hospital stays and specialist visits, take their place.
- A Medicare Advantage plan's cost structure, generally per-visit copayments or coinsurance, replaces the Part A and Part B costs. (Review your plan's Evidence of Coverage [EOC] for complete details on coverage and costs.) However, the Original Medicare costs set the bar for Medicare Advantage plans. They can charge no more for a given service than Part A or Part B does.

Medicare Advantage was dubbed Part C; however, it appears that title may be disappearing. Medicare Advantage isn't really a part; it is a package that provides hospital, medical, and prescription drug coverage.

Observation Status: When a Hospital Stay Is Not a Hospital Admission

You're in a hospital bed, eating hospital meals, seeing hospital physicians. But guess what? You may not be an inpatient. You could be on observation status.

Observation status is a way to monitor a patient whose condition is uncertain. The physician needs more time to determine whether to admit the patient or discharge him or her with further testing and treatment as an outpatient. Here's how this works.

Renee went to the ER with chest pain and shortness of breath. She was transferred from the ER to a hospital bed on observation status. Further testing and observation will determine how serious her condition is.

Renee likely won't recognize any difference in the care. But for Medicare beneficiaries, there are some huge differences. She was not admitted and is considered to be an outpatient. These are the ramifications.

- *The hospital bills all medical care and diagnostic tests under Part B.*
  With the Original Medicare Path, Renee will be subject to the Part B deductible and 20 percent coinsurance. A Medigap policy would help cover those costs.

If she opted for the Medicare Advantage Path, Renee would pay the plan's cost sharing for outpatient hospital coverage, which could be a copayment or coinsurance for every service.

- *Any medications fall under Part D coverage.*

  The hospital pharmacy is considered out-of-network for Part D drug coverage. Renee will likely have to submit a claim to her Part D insurer to get reimbursement for any drugs administered while on observation status. Her cost sharing may also be higher. And if the drugs she receives are not in her plan's formulary, her physician may need to request a formulary exception.

There is another concern. Medicare requires a three-day hospital admission before it will cover a stay in a skilled nursing facility (SNF).

Joann fractured her pelvis, and after three days in the hospital, she was admitted to an SNF for rehabilitation. However, she was never officially admitted to the hospital, so Medicare Part A would not cover her SNF stay. Medicare Advantage plans can choose to waive the three-day stay. Check the plan's EOC.

Because of rule changes in 2017, beneficiaries should not be shocked to learn about observation status after the fact. Hospitals must now furnish the Medicare Outpatient Observation Notice (MOON) to those receiving observation services for more than 24 hours. The one million beneficiaries every year who receive care under observation status will now know, in real time, about the cost implications and ongoing care concerns. If there is a possibility an SNF stay may be needed, they should discuss the plan with their physicians.

Skilled Nursing Facility (SNF) Stays
Medicare Basics

An SNF is basically a nursing home that has been certified by Medicare to provide follow-up care. Medicare has specific coverage criteria.

- You are admitted to the facility on a doctor's order for a medical condition that was treated during hospitalization.
- You must receive daily care that is provided by or under the supervision of skilled nursing or therapy staff. Rehabilitation after a stroke or a major automobile crash are examples.
- Medicare covers the first 20 days of a qualifying stay in an SNF. The average stay for those who qualify is 25 days.
- Coverage includes the facility, necessary skilled services, medications, meals, and medical social services.

Original Medicare Path

- Medicare has two specific criteria for coverage of an SNF stay.
  1. You must have a three-day inpatient hospital admission. (The discharge day does not count.)
  2. You must be admitted to the facility within 30 days of the hospital discharge.
- You are responsible for a copayment for days 21–100, $194.50 in 2022.

Medicare Advantage Path

- Medicare Advantage plans cover the first 20 days, and then cost sharing depends on the plan.
- The charge can never be more than what Original Medicare charges.

- A plan can choose to waive the three-day inpatient stay.
- As with most services, an in-network facility will be the most cost-effective option.
- Prior authorization requirements can apply.

Home Health Care
Medicare Basics

Part A covers most home health services that are provided by Medicare-certified home health care agencies. There are very specific criteria, but here are a few important points.

- You must be under the care of a doctor who creates and reviews a plan of care.
- Home care services must be medically necessary to treat the effects of an illness or injury.
- Your physician must certify that you need either skilled nursing care or therapy services that meet Medicare's home health criteria.
- Your physician must also certify that you are home-bound, generally unable to leave home because of the effects of the medical condition.
- Medicare will also cover medical social services and home health aide services for a patient who is receiving skilled care.

Original Medicare Path
- If you qualify, Medicare covers the services with no cost sharing.
- You can receive services from any Medicare-certified home health agency.
- Part B can pay for some of the services, although the deductible and coinsurance do not apply. The criteria are the same, and patients will not notice any differences.

Medicare Advantage Path
- There is no cost sharing for home care services provided by an in-network agency.
- Plans that offer out-of-network coverage may charge if you choose an agency that is not in the network.
- Prior authorization rules can apply, which means the plan can limit the number of visits.

Hospice
Medicare Basics
Hospice is holistic end-of-life care for the terminally ill. An interdisciplinary team works with the patient and family so that a person's last days may be spent with dignity and quality.

Here is what you should know.

- A hospice physician and the patient's primary physician, if available, must certify that the individual is terminally ill, with a medical prognosis of six months or less. (There is recertification if the patient lives longer than that.)
- The patient must elect palliative care. This is comfort care that focuses on pain relief and symptom management, not cures.
- Hospice patients can receive care in their homes, an assisted-living facility or nursing home, a hospital, or a hospice facility. The hospice benefit does not cover room and board.
- Part A also covers medications related to the terminal condition.
- If the hospice patient needs care unrelated to the medical condition, then other parts of Medicare would cover that. For instance, if a cancer patient sprains his ankle, Part B would cover the treatment, and Part D,

prescription drug coverage, would take care of the pain medication.

Original Medicare Path

- There is no deductible for hospice services.
- The only cost a beneficiary will face is a 5 percent co-insurance for each hospice-related drug and inpatient respite care, providing a break for caregivers.
- You can receive services from any Medicare-certified hospice.

Medicare Advantage Path

At this time, Medicare Advantage plans cannot provide hospice services. Terminally ill beneficiaries who elect this coverage will receive hospice care under Part A through a Medicare-certified hospice. But that may change in the future. (See chap. 6, "Questions and Answers about Part A and Part B Services.")

If those in hospice need care unrelated to their terminal illness, they must follow the plan's rules.

Part B, Medical Insurance

Part B, the outpatient component of Medicare, covers two types of services:

1. Medically necessary services or supplies that meet accepted standards of medicine and are needed to diagnose or treat an illness, an injury, a condition, a disease, or its symptoms, and
2. Preventive services, including screenings, checkups, and counseling to prevent illnesses, diseases, or other health problems.

Medically Necessary Services
Physician Services
This is one of the most important Part B benefits for Medicare beneficiaries.

Medicare Basics
- Several types of doctors can provide services under Part B, including these:
  - doctor of medicine, MD,
  - doctor of osteopathic medicine, DO,
  - doctor of podiatric medicine, DPM,
  - doctor of optometry, OD, and
  - doctor of chiropractic medicine, DC.
- There are specific rules for different types of physician services. For example, Medicare will pay for podiatry services for those who have diabetes-related nerve damage or need treatment for foot problems, such as bunion deformities and heel spurs.
- Part B also covers the services provided by physician assistants, nurse practitioners, clinical social workers, physical therapists, occupational therapists, speech-language pathologists, registered dietitians, and clinical psychologists.

Original Medicare Path
There are three types of health care providers.

1. *Participating providers:* These doctors and others must follow the process established by Centers for Medicare and Medicaid Services (CMS) and apply to become a provider who accepts Medicare assignment. They submit claims to Medicare and agree to accept Medicare's established payment.
   Here's what you should know about participating providers.

- You would be responsible for the Part B annual deductible ($233 in 2022) and then a 20 percent coinsurance. Only Medigap Plan C and Plan F cover the deductible. Any Medigap plan covers the coinsurance.
- You can find providers who accept assignment in the Physician Compare database at www.medicare-links.com/physician-compare.
- According to the Kaiser Family Foundation, about 99 percent of nonpediatric providers accept Medicare assignment.

2. *Nonparticipating providers:* These providers haven't signed an agreement to accept assignment but will see Medicare patients on a case-by-case basis. They reserve the right to charge up to 15 percent more than the Medicare-approved amount, known as Part B excess charges. Only about 5 percent of physicians apply these charges, and they tend to be specialists in urban areas.

Here's what you should know about nonparticipating providers.

- You might have to pay at the time of services.
- Your doctor is supposed to file a claim with Medicare. If that doesn't happen, ask the doctor to file one. If there are problems, call 1 (800) MEDICARE to discuss this.
- In some cases, you may have to file a claim for reimbursement. (This is called the Patient's Request for Medical Payment [www.medicare-links.com/patients-request-for-medical-payment].)
- An optional Medigap benefit, Part B excess charges, can cover the surcharge.
- There is a very small percentage of providers, less than 3 percent, in this category.
- Connecticut, Massachusetts, Minnesota, New York, Ohio, Pennsylvania, Rhode Island, and Vermont do not allow excess charges.

3. *Providers who have opted out:* Physicians can opt out of the Medicare program entirely and become private contracting physicians. They must establish contracts with their patients and can bill them whatever amount they determine is appropriate. Of note, providers who have opted out of the Medicare program must opt out for all their Medicare patients.

Here's what to know about opted-out providers.

- You must sign the contract and agree to pay the entire cost of any services.
- Neither the physician nor you will get reimbursement from Medicare.
- A Medigap policy will not pay for any of these services.
- According to the Kaiser Family Foundation, less than 1 percent of physicians have opted out of Medicare.

Medicare Advantage Path

- With some plans, you will need referrals to see physicians other than your primary.
- Many plans also require prior authorization for seeing other physicians.
- Physician services will apply toward the health plan deductible, if the plan has one.
- You will be responsible for any copayment or coinsurance.
- The plan controls the delivery of physician services through provider networks. (Please review chapter 5, "Shopping for a Medicare Advantage Plan," if you have questions about networks.) Out-of-network services will cost more. A network can change at any time. Doctors you see one year may not be in-network the next year.

Other Outpatient Services
Medicare Basics
There are many other outpatient services on the Part B list. Some of the more common ones include the following.

- acupuncture,*
- ambulance services,
- chiropractic services,*
- diabetic supplies,*
- diagnostic tests and procedures,
- dialysis,
- drugs,*
- intravenous therapy,
- medical equipment, such as walkers, crutches, and wheelchairs,
- oxygen,
- outpatient services, including physical therapy, occupational therapy, speech-language pathology services, radiation therapy, and dialysis, to name a few, and
- telehealth services.*
  (See the following sections for more details about services with *.)

Original Medicare Path
- Just as with physician services, the Part B deductible and 20 percent coinsurance apply to these medically necessary services. A Medigap policy can help with these costs.
- You will need to use an approved supplier for equipment and supplies. In December 2020, CMS introduced a supplier directory. Find it at www.medicare-links.com/medical-supplier-directory.
- There can be prior authorization requirements for a few outpatient procedures. Some equipment, like power mobility devices and pressure-reducing mattresses, requires authorization.

Medicare Advantage Path
- Once again, remember that coverage rules, referrals, prior authorization, and networks may apply.
- Your best option is to get Part B services from an in-network provider.
- Check out the costs you will face. You will need to pay the medical plan's deductible and cost sharing. Know that just about every plan charges a 20 percent coinsurance for chemotherapy or dialysis.

Here's a look at some Part B services that tend to raise questions.

Acupuncture
Medicare Basics
Acupuncture is a treatment in which practitioners stimulate specific points on the body, most often by inserting thin needles through the skin. In 2020, Medicare started covering all types of acupuncture, including dry needling, for the treatment of chronic low back pain as an alternative to opioid medications.

- To qualify, a patient must have had chronic low back pain for 12 weeks or longer with no systemic cause and pain that is not associated with surgery.
- Medicare will cover up to 12 sessions in 90 days, with an additional eight sessions for those patients who demonstrate improvement.
- Treatments must be administered by a doctor or a physician's assistant, nurse practitioner, or health care professional with a master's or doctorate level training in acupuncture and a state license to practice acupuncture.

Original Medicare Path

- Medicare does not cover acupuncture for any condition other than chronic low back pain.
- As with any service, you can see providers who accept Medicare assignment.
- The Part B deductible and coinsurance will apply.

Medicare Advantage Path

- You may have to choose a provider in-network.
- Referral and prior authorization requirements, along with a deductible and copayment or coinsurance, may apply.
- Some plans will cover acupuncture for other medical conditions.

Chiropractic Services

Medicare Basics

A chiropractor or other qualified professional must perform manual manipulation of the spine to correct subluxation—that is, when one or more spinal vertebrae are out of alignment—as documented by an exam or X-ray.

Original Medicare Path

- The chiropractor must accept Medicare assignment, and typical Part B cost sharing applies.
- As long as the services are medically necessary, there is no limit on visits.

Medicare Advantage Path

- The plan's cost sharing, network, and referral requirements can apply.
- Prior authorization may limit the number of visits.
- A plan may cover the services for reasons other than subluxation.

Diabetic Supplies
Medicare Basics
Part B covers many of the supplies a diabetic beneficiary may need:

- blood glucose (sugar) self-testing equipment and supplies for those who use or don't use insulin (the amount of supplies may vary),
- blood glucose monitors and all the necessary supplies, including test strips, lancets, and glucose control solutions (for checking the accuracy of testing supplies), and
- insulin pumps and the insulin used with a pump.

Part D, prescription drug coverage, is responsible for insulin not used with pumps and the necessary insulin administration supplies, including syringes or pens, needles, alcohol swabs, and gauze.

Original Medicare Path
- You must order supplies from a pharmacy or medical supplier that's enrolled in Medicare and accepts assignment.
- You will need a doctor's prescription.
- The pharmacy and supplier must submit claims for testing supplies to Medicare; you cannot do that.

Medicare Advantage Path
Plans can specify the brand of monitors and test strips, along with authorization requirements. The plan's EOC will have all the details.

Drugs
Medicare Basics
Part B covers drugs in very specific situations. These are some of the more common ones:

- intravenous or injectable drugs (those that are not usually self-administered) administered in a clinic or office by a physician part of a plan,

- immunosuppressive drugs for Medicare transplant patients,
- oral anti-nausea medications used within 48 hours of chemotherapy as a replacement for IV drugs, and
- parenteral nutrition (administered through a vein).

Original Medicare Path
As with other services, health care providers must accept assignment, and Part B cost sharing applies.

Medicare Advantage Path
- Seeing providers in-network will save money.
- Know about the prior authorization requirements.
- Most plans charge a 20 percent coinsurance for Part B drugs.
- Plans may also apply step therapy to Part B drug administration. The patient may have to try condition-based preferred medications before using more expensive drugs. Each plan establishes its procedures.

Telehealth Services
Most beneficiaries don't realize that Medicare has covered telehealth for over 20 years. It started out as a benefit for rural patients only but then expanded to those with an acute stroke, with a substance disorder, or on dialysis. During the COVID pandemic, telehealth became a hot topic because we were sheltering in place. In response, Medicare expanded telehealth benefits.

Medicare Basics
- Telehealth services include office visits, psychotherapy, consultations, and certain other medical or health services provided by a doctor or health care provider using audio and video communication technology.
- Medicare also covers virtual check-ins (brief calls) and e-visits (talks instead of visits).

Original Medicare Path
You will pay the same as if you were visiting your health care providers.

Medicare Advantage Path
- Starting in 2020, Medicare Advantage plans have been able to provide more telehealth services than Original Medicare.
- Plans can require authorization.

Medicare's Response to the COVID Pandemic

We all know how our lives and livelihoods were disrupted by COVID for two years, and we're not going to revisit that. However, since this is a book about Medicare, let's review Medicare's response.

- Medicare ensured that Part A, Part B, and Medicare Advantage plans covered the necessary care for those stricken with COVID.
- Medicare Advantage plans had to:
  ○ waive prior authorization requirements and cost sharing for services to address the outbreak, and
  ○ cover in-network and out-of-network services in the same way and at the same cost.
- Part D drug coverage relaxed restrictions on refill limits and home or mail delivery of drugs, waived prior authorization, and reimbursed costs for out-of-network drugs.
- Medicare expanded telehealth services for beneficiaries.

As we get to a new normal, Medicare will reevaluate these measures to determine whether any of them will continue. But going forward, we know that Medicare will pay for COVID vaccinations and testing.

Preventive Services

Besides covering reasonable and necessary services, Part B also covers many preventive services. For most of these, there is no cost to the beneficiary. Each service has its own specific coverage criteria, so for information, check the list at www.medicare-links.com/medicares-preventive -services.

Here are some important points to know about some of the more common preventive services.

Colonoscopies
Medicare Basics
- This is a preventive service with no cost to the beneficiary.
- Medicare covers this test once every 10 years or every 2 years for those at high risk for colorectal cancer (those with a family or personal history of the disease or inflammatory bowel disease).
- If the physician removes a polyp or takes a biopsy, the procedure is diagnostic.

Original Medicare Path
The Part B coinsurance applies to diagnostic colonoscopies but not the deductible.

Medicare Advantage Path
- Plans must cover preventive colonoscopies without applying deductibles, copayments, or coinsurance when seeing an in-network provider.
- Authorization may be necessary.
- Cost sharing could apply to a diagnostic procedure.

Mammograms

Medicare Basics

- Part B covers one baseline mammogram for women ages 35–39 and a screening mammogram once every 12 months for women age 40 or older.
- Women with medical issues, such as a history of cancer, can qualify for diagnostic mammograms more frequently than once a year.

Original Medicare Path

- There is no cost for a screening mammogram when seeing providers who accept assignment.
- The Part B deductible and coinsurance apply to a diagnostic test.

Medicare Advantage Path

A plan cannot charge for a screening mammogram, but cost sharing, along with network rules and prior authorization, can apply to a diagnostic one.

Prostate Cancer Screenings

Medicare Basics

Part B covers digital rectal exams and prostate specific antigen (PSA) blood tests once every 12 months for men over 50.

Original Medicare Path

There is no cost for the yearly PSA test; however, the Part B deductible and coinsurance apply to the rectal exam.

Medicare Advantage Path

There can be no copayment for the PSA test. Check the plan's details for information about the rectal exam.

Vaccinations

Every Medicare beneficiary needs vaccinations. Both Part B and Part D cover vaccinations. This section discusses the ones that fall under Part B. (See chap. 6, "Part D, Prescription Drug Coverage," for information about Part D vaccines.)

Medicare Basics

Part B covers most vaccines that Medicare beneficiaries need. Regardless of the Medicare path, there will be no copayment or deductible for these vaccinations.

- COVID-19: Medicare will cover the initial vaccination and booster shots.
- Influenza virus: Medicare covers this vaccination once a year for all beneficiaries.
- Pneumococcal pneumonia:
  - There are two vaccines, Prevnar 13 and Pneumovax 23.
  - Once enrolled, Medicare will cover the first vaccination at any time and the second one if it's administered at least one year later.
- Hepatitis B:
  - Part B covers this vaccine for those at medium or high risk for the disease. This includes those with hemophilia, end-stage renal disease (ESRD), or diabetes and health care workers who have frequent contact with blood and bodily fluids.
  - The vaccine involves a series of three shots over a six-month period.
- Other vaccines directly related to the treatment of an injury or direct exposure to a disease or condition: Examples include anti-rabies treatment, tetanus vaccination, botulism antitoxin, and immune globulin.

Original Medicare Path

You can get the vaccines from any doctor or pharmacy that accepts Medicare assignment.

Medicare Advantage Path
You will likely have to visit a doctor or pharmacy in the plan's network.

Wellness Visits

The Affordable Care Act (ACA) introduced two wellness visits that focus on prevention of disease and detection of depression, safety issues, and cognitive impairment.

Medicare Basics
The first is a Welcome to Medicare preventive visit. This introductory visit, within the first 12 months that you have Part B, reviews your medical and social history and provides counseling about preventive services. Specifically, this visit includes the following:

- height, weight, and blood pressure measurements,
- a calculation of your body mass index,
- a simple vision test,
- a review of your risk factors for depression, functional ability and safety level, and current opioid prescriptions,
- screenings for visual acuity and potential substance use disorders,
- education, counseling, and referrals based on the previous components,
- a written plan addressing screenings, vaccinations, and other preventive services, and
- end-of-life planning (if you consent).

If you don't make an appointment for this visit by the 13th month that you have Part B, you've missed your opportunity.

The second preventive service is a Medicare Wellness Visit every 12 months to update your personalized prevention plan. The visit includes the following:

- a review of your medical and family history,
- height, weight, blood pressure, and other routine measurements,
- a detection of any cognitive impairment,
- personalized health advice,
- updating your list of current providers, suppliers, prescriptions, and health risk factors and the schedule for appropriate preventive services, and
- advance care planning.

There is no cost for these two wellness services. However, if the physician addresses a medical issue, the visit could be considered diagnostic, and Part B costs could apply.

Original Medicare Path
Remember to see providers who accept assignment.

Medicare Advantage Path
Schedule your appointment in-network, most likely with your primary physician.

Questions and Answers about Part A and Part B Services

How do I replace a lost Medicare card?

You can request a replacement card through your *my* Social Security account.

1. Log into your account. You'll need to enter the security code Social Security sends to you electronically.
2. Select "Replacement Documents" and then "Mail my replacement Medicare card."

The new card should arrive by mail within 30 days.

If you need your Medicare number sooner than that, click on the "Benefit Verification Letter" link on the same page. You can download or print the PDF.

How can I find a Medicare-certified hospice or home care agency?

Go to the same website for finding Medicare physicians at www.medicare-links.com/physician-compare. Pull down the menu in the "Provider Type" box, and you'll find the link to hospice or home health agencies.

How does a deductible work in Medicare plans?

Many beneficiaries who choose the Original Medicare Path will face the Part A hospital deductible and the Part B deductible. Medigap Plan F and Plan G have high-deductible versions. Medicare Advantage plans can have a health deductible and every Medical Savings Account plan has one. Here are some points about the deductible for medical services.

- The deductible is the amount you must pay out-of-pocket before the plan starts paying its share.
- Only the amount you pay for covered services counts toward the deductible.
- Once you've paid the deductible, you'll be responsible for the plan's designated cost sharing, either copayments or coinsurance.
- The deductible resets every calendar year.
- A higher deductible requires the beneficiary to pay more out-of-pocket, but the premiums are generally lower.

Part D drug coverage can also have a deductible.

Does Medicare cover palliative care?

Palliative care is specialized medical care for people living with a serious illness. It focuses on providing relief from the symptoms and stress, no matter the diagnosis or stage of the disease. The goal is to improve the quality of life for both the patient and the family.

Palliative care is an important component of hospice; however, it can also be provided along with curative care for those who have chronic conditions, such as cancer, heart failure, or lung disease.

Medicare does not have a specific program for palliative care. However, many of the treatments and services are reasonable and necessary to treat a serious illness and would be covered for that reason, as in these two situations.

> Ruthann was receiving palliative care to deal with the effects of chemotherapy and cancer.

> Jose was recuperating from a traumatic industrial accident and needed palliative care for pain control.

As you have read several times, coverage depends on the Medicare path. Those with the Original Medicare Path should see providers who accept assignment and will be responsible for the Part B cost sharing. With the Medicare Advantage Path, the coverage rules (networks, referrals, prior authorization) and cost sharing can apply.

Will Medicare Advantage plans ever cover hospice services?

Under the current regulations, a Medicare Advantage member who needs hospice care will receive the services under Part A from a Medicare-certified hospice. But that may change.

In 2021, CMS started a three-year demonstration project to test the inclusion of hospice services in Medicare Advantage plans. In the first year, 53 plans participated.

So the answer to this question is "Stay tuned."

What should I know about concierge physicians?

Some physicians are turning to concierge practice models, also called retainer-based or direct primary care. They charge their patients annual membership fees that Medicare does not cover. However, there are benefits to being a member, such as spending more time with the doctor or getting same-day appointments.

Concierge physicians' fees typically do not cover emergency care, hospitalizations, evaluations by other physicians or specialists, outside lab work, pathology services, radiology, or physical therapy.

If the doctor has opted out of Medicare, all services are on a contract basis for those who chose the Original Medicare Path. Neither the physician nor the beneficiary can get reimbursement from Medicare.

A Medicare Advantage plan will not cover the membership fee. If the doctor is in-network, the plan covers medically necessary services.

Recognizing that Medicare Advantage networks can change at any time, what are some tips to make sure I can get the medical care I need?

- Know how to access your plan's provider directory. In most cases, you can find this somewhere on the plan's website.
- Choose your primary physician carefully. In some plans, your choice may mean you are also choosing the providers and hospitals associated with that doctor.

- Any time you make an appointment, confirm your health care provider is in-network.
- If your plan allows you to see out-of-network health care providers, confirm that they will submit claims to your plan. They are under no obligation to do so.
- Be flexible. If the network changes, your Medicare Advantage plan must ensure that you have access to necessary services, which can mean continuing care with new providers.

What is a benefit period?

This is a key part of the payment structure for Original Medicare. A benefit period begins the day of admission to a hospital or SNF and can cover 60 days. It ends when there have been no hospitalizations or SNF stays for 60 days. If there is another hospital or SNF stay in the same calendar year, a new benefit period begins. You would be responsible for the deductibles, copayments, or coinsurance for each benefit period, possibly paying these costs more than once in a year.

Depending on the number of days between admissions, there may be more than one benefit period.

> Maria was hospitalized January 7–13 and paid the Part A deductible ($1,556 for 2022). She was readmitted on April 1. Because this was more than 60 days after discharge in January, she was subject to another Part A deductible for the second hospital stay.

However, another admission within 60 days of the previous discharge is part of the same benefit period.

Maria was discharged from the second hospitalization on April 15. After a fall on May 3, she was re-admitted for three days. Because this stay was less than 60 days from the last discharge in April, it is in the same benefit period, so Maria did not have to pay the deductible again.

Days 61–90 come into play if a person doesn't stay out of the hospital or SNF for 60 days.

Because of complications, Maria was in and out of the hospital over the next four months. These re-peat admissions extended the benefit period, cov-ered by the deductible she paid in April. (She was never out of the hospital for 60 days.) On August 29, she was admitted for her 61st day, and the per-day copayments came into play ($389 in 2022).

What are lifetime reserve days?

These are 60 days that a beneficiary can use above the 90 al-lowed by Part A. There are so many nuances to using these reserve days that the CMS dedicates an entire chapter (14 pages) to the topic in its Medicare Benefit Policy Manual. But, in simplest terms, if someone has repeated admissions to a hospital or SNF, it's possible that the inpatient stays could total more than 90 days in a very extended benefit period.

Maria's complications led to more hospitalizations throughout the rest of the year. When her inpatient days since April totaled 91 (without being out of the hospital for at least 60 days), she could decide to use lifetime reserve days.

These days can be used once—the reason these are called lifetime reserve days—and only at the beneficiary's direction. Most Medigap policies offer 365 additional lifetime reserve days. Be sure to get all the details and understand your options.

What are the chances I will need to use my lifetime reserve days?

I read recently that a man was hospitalized for 500 days after being diagnosed with COVID. However, it's possible you may not use those days, and here are some reasons why.

- Health care is evolving and moving to outpatient care. In 1982, Medicare reimbursed only about 200 procedures in an ambulatory setting, so all the rest had to be done in the hospital setting. By 2016, more than 3,400 outpatient procedures were approved.

  Now CMS has started the process to phase out its inpatient-only list, meaning Medicare will cover more outpatient procedures.
- Hospital stays are decreasing. For example, between 2005 and 2014, the number of hospital stays for those 75 years or older dropped almost 12 percent.
- The length of hospital stays is also decreasing. According to the Centers for Disease Control and Prevention (CDC), in 1980, 65- to 84-year-olds stayed in a hospital, on average, almost 12 days. In 2018, that number was 5.2 days.
- In some cases, repeated hospitalizations may relate to a medical condition that requires hospice or palliative care, which can be provided in a nonhospital setting.

Will Medicare cover vitamin B_{12} injections?

That depends on the reason for the injection. Part B will cover vitamin B_{12} injections for those diagnosed with specific medical conditions, such as pernicious or macrocytic anemia, gastrectomy, and neuropathy due to malnutrition. Medicare doesn't cover vitamin B_{12} for generalized weakness or fatigue.

Talk with your physician about your concerns.

Where can I find an approved supplier for diabetic supplies, equipment, or the like?

If you have coverage through the Original Medicare Path, check the database at www.medicare-links.com/medical-supplier-directory. For those with the Medicare Advantage Path, check the plan's information or ask a plan representative.

Can I get free diabetic supplies from the company I see on television?

If you see a TV advertisement that promises to send supplies automatically, change the channel. Medicare won't pay for supplies unless you order them. Nothing can be sent automatically.

Also, if you get a call from someone offering free diabetic supplies, hang up. You would have to provide personal information, like your Social Security number.

Does Medicare cover an annual physical exam?

Federal statute prohibits Medicare from paying for annual physical examinations. However, the ACA introduced Medicare's version, called the Initial Preventive Physical Examination. However, unlike annual physicals, you get only one of these visits, and it does not resemble a physical exam. There is no palpation (feeling with fingers or hands), no auscultation (listening to body sounds), and no percussion (tapping body parts), all essential components of a physical examination.

Because "physical examination" is in the regulatory title, there was (and still is) considerable confusion. Medicare probably recognized that, and now on the Medicare.gov website, this service is called the Welcome to Medicare preventive visit. (See more about this visit in chapter 6, "Part B, Medical Insurance.")

The annual Wellness Visit, another preventive service, may be annual, but it, too, is not a physical exam.

If you chose the Original Medicare Path, you could still get a physical exam, but you may have to pay for it. However, Part B would cover an EKG for the diagnosis of an abnormal heart rhythm or a chest X-ray to assess severe lung congestion, with the usual cost sharing.

Some Medicare Advantage plans offer routine physical exams, generally when performed by the primary physician. Check the plan's EOC for more information.

Other Coverage Concerns

Dental and Vision
Medicare Basics

Medicare's coverage of dental and vision services is very limited.

Medicare will pay for dental services in the following situations:

- services that are part of a covered procedure, such as reconstruction of the jaw following an accident or extractions done in preparation for radiation treatments of the jaw, and
- oral examinations preceding a kidney transplantation or heart valve replacement, under certain circumstances.

On the vision side, Medicare covers these services:

- cataract surgery using traditional surgical techniques or lasers,
- glaucoma tests for those at high risk,

- eye exams for those with diabetic retinopathy, and
- certain diagnostic tests and treatment for age-related macular degeneration.

Medicare also provides a nominal allowance for glasses or contact lenses after cataract surgery.

Medicare does not cover routine dental services, such as cleanings, fillings, tooth extractions, dentures, or other dental devices, or routine vision services, including eye exams, refractions, eyeglasses, and contact lenses.

Original Medicare Path

- The Part B deductible and 20 percent coinsurance apply to covered services.
- You will need to receive services from a provider who accepts assignment.
- You can investigate dental or vision plans if you need coverage for routine services. There are different levels of benefits and premiums. You can get this coverage at any time. Some insurers offer Medigap policies that include dental and vision benefits, generally for a higher premium.

Medicare Advantage Path

- For medically necessary services, the usual plan rules and cost sharing apply.
- Many plans incorporate routine dental and vision services for no extra premium.
- The coverage can vary depending on the plan. Some plans offer only preventive dental services, such as oral exams, cleanings, dental X-rays, and fluoride treatments. Other plans provide comprehensive dental to maintain and treat problems, including fillings, extractions, and root canals. Many plans offer a mix of the two services.
- The EOC details the plan's criteria. There can be exclusions and limits on the frequency and dollar value of treatments.

- In-network care is the best option.
- Plans can also provide an opportunity to upgrade the services for an additional premium.
- Find out how payment works for these services. If you use network providers, the plan may pay the providers directly. Some plans have a reimbursement allowance. You can see any provider, but you would have to pay the bill and then submit receipts.

Hearing Exams and Hearing Aids
Medicare Basics
Almost 50 percent of those who are 75 and older have disabling hearing loss. However, fewer than 30 percent have ever used a hearing aid. One big reason for that: Medicare does not cover hearing aids or exams to fit hearing aids.

As with dental and vision services, Medicare offers limited coverage, paying for hearing and balance exams to determine whether medical treatment is necessary. The exam may determine that hearing loss is due to a medical condition, such as chronic ear infections or Paget's disease. However, when hearing loss is related to aging or heredity, Medicare does not cover the tests or hearing aids.

Original Medicare Path
- The Part B deductible and 20 percent coinsurance apply for any services that meet Medicare coverage criteria as noted under Medicare Basics.
- You will need to receive those medically necessary services from a provider who accepts Medicare assignment.
- If you believe hearing aids are in your future, start a fund.

Medicare Advantage Path
- Some plans offer hearing tests and hearing aids.
- Check the evidence of coverage for details. For instance, the plan will pay $400 for a hearing aid or offer a benefit

amount, such as $2,500, for an exam, fitting, and hearing aid.

- You'll likely need to obtain prior authorization and use the plan's hearing aid provider.

Travel within the United States
Medicare Basics

Just about everyone plans to travel once they retire. So there are questions about Medicare coverage if something happens away from home.

- No matter where you travel in the United States or its territories, Medicare, no matter your path, will cover any emergency.
- However, routine or nonemergency medical care depends on the specific coverage you have.
- If a pharmacy has a national presence and a contract with your plan, your prescription drug coverage will work anywhere in the United States.

Original Medicare Path

- You can see any health care provider who accepts Medicare assignment for routine care wherever you are in the United States or its territories. Visit the Physician Compare database to find one.
- The usual Part A and Part B cost sharing will apply.

Medicare Advantage Path

- Plans that do not offer out-of-network coverage, such as an HMO (health maintenance organization), will pay for emergencies but most likely not follow-up care. You can either stay at your destination and pay out-of-pocket or travel back home and receive care in-network.

    Margaret rented a condo for three months in Florida to get away from winter in her state. The second day there, she broke her shoulder. Her HMO paid for emergency treatment but would not cover physical therapy. She opted to fly home for three weeks to get the essential therapy.

- PPO (preferred provider organization) and some other plans will cover out-of-network care. Remember, health care providers have no obligation to see these patients, and you will likely pay more.

  Rick was injured in a car crash out of state. His PPO plan covered the emergency surgery, hospitalization, and follow-up care. By the time he flew home, he had hit the plan's maximum out-of-pocket limit, $10,000.

- Check your plan's EOC for details. It may cover travel within the United States.

CDC Recommendations for Drugs That Travel with You out of the Country

No matter where you go, it's smart to pack your prescription medications, not only what you'll need but an emergency backup supply, in a carry-on bag. The CDC has these tips for international travel.

- Keep medicines in their original containers and clearly labeled with your full passport name, doctor's name, drug name, and dosage.
- Bring copies of all prescriptions for medicines.
- Pack a note on letterhead stationery from the prescribing doctor for controlled substances and injectable medicines, such as EpiPens.

Visit the CDC website at www.medicare-links.com/cdc -resources-for-travelers for traveler advice.

Foreign Travel
Medicare Basics
Except in a few limited situations, Medicare won't pay for any health care or supplies you get outside the 50 states, the District of Columbia, Puerto Rico, the U.S. Virgin Islands, Guam, American Samoa, and the Northern Mariana Islands. Here are two situations Medicare will cover.

- You're in the United States when you have a medical emergency and a foreign hospital is closer than the nearest U.S. hospital.
- You need medical care, even if it is not an emergency, on a cruise ship that is less than six hours away from a U.S. port.

Part D drug plans don't cover prescription medications outside the United States.

Original Medicare Path
Medicare doesn't otherwise cover this care. However, some Medigap policies provide coverage for foreign travel emergencies. The policy will pay up to 80 percent of the cost of emergency care abroad, with a deductible of no more than $250 and up to $50,000 in a lifetime. Your situation must meet the policy's conditions, which include the following.

- The care you receive is medically necessary.
- The care begins during the first 60 days of your travel. (This Medigap benefit is not meant to provide medical care for those who live in a foreign country for more than two months.)

Check the Medigap policy's information for specifics.

Medicare Advantage Path

- As with any Part A or Part B service, these plans must provide the same coverage outside the United States, as noted under Medicare Basics.
- Some plans do offer coverage beyond that, so review the EOC or talk with a plan representative.

Questions and Answers about Other Coverage

Will Medicare cover the lens implant that is part of my cataract surgery?

Medicare Part B will cover a single-focus (monofocal) intra-ocular lens. This lens will provide clear distance vision, but you will need glasses for near and intermediate vision.

Those who need cataract surgery now have the option of a multifocal lens that will correct distance vision, near vision, and all distances in between and one that will correct astigmatism. Medicare has approved these lenses but does not cover the full cost. You will have to pay the additional costs related to these lenses, which can start around $1,500.

What should I do if I plan to move to a new city two years after enrolling in Medicare?

The first thing on your to-do list should be to notify Social Security about your change in address.

1. Log into your *my* Social Security account.
2. Click "Go to My Profile."
3. Click on "Update Contact Information," and enter your new address.
4. Call Social Security at (800) 772-1213 if you have any problems.

If you chose the Original Medicare Path, know these two points.

- You will need to enroll in a new drug plan.
  - Do this from a month before to two months after your move.
  - Find a new plan through the Medicare Plan Finder, and then contact the plan to enroll.
  - If it turns out your current drug plan works the best in your new location, you still need to contact the plan because there can be a change in the premium and pharmacy network.
- In most cases, your Medigap policy will move with you.
  - Notify the insurance company about your change in address. There may be a rate adjustment.
  - If you want to enroll in a new plan, check with the sponsor of the policy to see whether you can get a different one. You may have to answer some medical questions.
  - If you move to a state like Wisconsin that has its own standardization model for Medigap policies, you may need to switch policies. Contact your Medigap insurer or check with the state insurance commissioner.

If you elected Medicare Advantage and you are moving out of the plan's service area, you have the opportunity to pick the coverage of your choice. (See chap. 3, "Changing Paths down the Road.")

That could be another Medicare Advantage plan. Or you would have a guaranteed issue right to get a Medigap policy. You can also enroll in a Part D drug plan. Generally, you have one month before you move up until two months after you move to make a change.

How does a hospital in a foreign country get paid for emergency care?

Foreign hospitals don't submit claims, so you will need to pay for the services and then file a claim for reimbursement.

- In the rare case that Medicare would cover an emergency outside the United States, you will need to submit a claim to Medicare for services. Find the form at www.medicare-links.com/patients-request-for-medical-payment.
- If you have benefits through either a Medigap policy or Medicare Advantage plan, complete the claim form provided by the insurance company, attach the receipts, and send it to the designated address.
- As with anything else, keep copies for your file.

Part D, Prescription Drug Coverage

You're all enrolled in Medicare and have prescription drug coverage. It doesn't matter whether that's a stand-alone prescription drug plan or a Medicare Advantage plan with prescription drug coverage (MA-PD plan); Part D works the same. There are some things to know, since you will have to live with drug coverage for a long time.

Part D Terminology

You were introduced to some terms in chapter 5, "Shopping for Part D, Prescription Drug Coverage." Here's a more complete list, all in one place.

Formulary: This is a list of medications a plan covers.

- There are certain drugs that every plan must cover, and then each plan decides additional ones it will cover. It's likely that no two formularies are identical.
- If you take any drugs that are not on the plan's formulary, you will pay the full cost.

- You have to pay attention because formularies can change, which means today your drug is covered, but tomorrow, it may not be.

Brand-name drug: This drug is sold under a specific name or trademark that is protected by a patent for several years.

- The company holding the patent is the only one that can produce and sell the drug, and there can be no generic version during that time.
- These tend to be the most expensive medications.

Generic drug: This chemical copy of a brand-name drug contains the same active ingredient but with different inactive ingredients.

- It is sold after the patent expires.
- The drug looks different, is sold under different names, and generally costs less.

Drug tier: This is how insurance companies group and price medications. Medicare drug plans can have up to six tiers.

- Tier 1, preferred generics: These are commonly prescribed, low-cost medications.
- Tier 2, nonpreferred generics: These are usually generic medications that cost more than Tier 1 drugs.
- Tier 3, preferred brands: These brand-name medications are listed on the formulary and are generally safe alternatives to more expensive brand-name drugs. For most, there are no generic alternatives available. Plans can charge a copayment or a coinsurance for these medications.
- Tier 4, nonpreferred brands: These brand-name drugs cost more than those in Tier 3. Sometimes that's because

there is a generic alternative available. Most drug plans charge a coinsurance for Tier 4 medications.

- Tier 5, specialty drugs: These drugs treat complex conditions, like cancer, diabetes, and multiple sclerosis. These can be either generic or brand name and are the most expensive medications in a formulary. Plans can charge between 25 percent and 33 percent for these medications.
- Tier 6, select care medications: Not every drug plan has this tier, which is limited to select generic medications to treat blood pressure, cholesterol, and diabetes.

Premium: This is the amount you can pay monthly for drug coverage.

- Stand-alone plans have premiums. In 2022, the premiums started around $7 and went up from there, with just a few plans over $100.
- Many Medicare Advantage plans do not charge an additional premium for drug coverage, but some plans do. The amount depends on the plan.

Deductible: This is the amount you pay out-of-pocket for drugs before the plan starts paying.

- Every year, Medicare sets the standard deductible. The 2022 deductible was $480.
- A plan can choose to charge no deductible or any amount up to the standard amount.

Copayment: This is the predetermined amount for a medication, such as $5 or $45, that the drug plan member pays out-of-pocket per prescription.

Coinsurance: A plan can charge a percentage of the cost of a medication, such as 30 percent, that you would pay out-of-pocket per prescription. If the cost of the drug goes up, the amount you pay also increases.

Noncovered drug: A plan can choose not to cover a specific drug. You would have to pay full price.

Coverage rules: A drug plan can put in place some requirements to control the use of medications for safety or cost reasons. There are three rules.

- Quantity limit: The plan limits the number of pills in a prescription, the number of prescriptions in a month, or the dosage strength.
- Prior authorization: The physician must obtain consent from the plan before prescribing a certain medication.
- Step therapy: Before ordering a certain medication (usually a very expensive one), the physician must prescribe a less expensive but proven-effective medication. If the individual experiences side effects or other problems, the physician can then "step up" to order the more costly drug.

Pharmacies: For Part D to cover your medication, you must deal with a network pharmacy. This is one that has agreed to provide drugs and supplies to those enrolled in the plan at a contracted price that is less than the full cost. However, just because a pharmacy is in-network doesn't mean it will be the best deal. Know about the different types of pharmacies.

- Standard retail pharmacy: Once known as nonpreferred, this in-network pharmacy offers covered drugs to members at the plan's negotiated price.
- Preferred retail pharmacy: This is an in-network pharmacy that offers covered drugs to plan members at lower out-of-pocket costs than what the members would pay at a standard retail pharmacy. Not every drug plan includes preferred pharmacies.

- Mail order: Most plans offer a mail-order program. You have the benefit of getting a three-month supply of your covered prescription drugs sent directly to your home. Years ago, you could have gotten three months for the price of two, but those days are gone. It is possible you could pay more for some drugs than at a retail pharmacy, so check your plan's cost sharing.
- Out-of-network pharmacy: This pharmacy does not have a contract with a particular plan. Avoid these, or you'll pay all costs.

A Grocery Store and Medications

You probably grew up during a time when your family got milk and bread at the grocery store and pills from the corner drugstore. Things certainly have changed. Many large-chain grocery stores have pharmacies that offer preferred retail cost sharing. If your grocery store has a pharmacy counter, check it out. You might save money that you can use on groceries.

Part D Drug Payment Stages

With the drug coverage you had prior to Medicare, you probably paid the same price for your drugs all year. Prepare for a change now that you have Medicare. Part D, prescription drug coverage, has four payment stages. There are different costs associated with each stage, so you could pay four different prices in a calendar year.

Here's a look at the payment stages.

1. *Deductible:* Every year, Medicare sets the standard deductible. In 2022, that was $480.

- This is the amount you pay out-of-pocket before the plan starts paying.
- A plan can choose to charge no deductible or any amount up to the standard amount.

2. *Initial Coverage:* By design, you'll pay 25 percent of the cost of medications in this stage, and the plan pays the rest.
   - Most plans choose to charge a copayment (a fixed amount, such as $3 or $10).
   - Once the amount that you and the plan have spent reaches a threshold ($4,430 in 2022), you'll enter the next stage.

3. *The Coverage Gap, a.k.a. the donut hole:* By design, you are responsible for most or all the costs in this stage.
   - However, now there are discounts, so you pay 25 percent of the cost of a drug. For some medications, you'll pay less then before, and for others, you'll pay more (think sticker shock.) (See "Facts about the Donut Hole" box.)
   - Once your true (total) out-of-pocket costs (what you've paid) reach another threshold ($7,550 in 2022), it's on to the last payment stage.

4. *Catastrophic Coverage:* Generally, you pay the greater of 5 percent or a set copayment for generic and brand-name drugs ($3.95 and $9.85 in 2022). There is no maximum amount or cap on how much you could pay in this stage.

Once the year ends, the cycle resets, and the costs are adjusted for the new year.

In each month you get prescriptions, the plan sponsor will send an Explanation of Benefits (EOB), which is a monthly prescription summary. That summary will note, among other things, refills you've gotten, the costs, and the drug plan payment stage you are in that month.

More about the Part D Deductible

Medicare prescription drug coverage, can be confusing, and much of that confusion starts with the deductible. Check out these important points.

- The deductible is the amount you must pay for covered drugs before the plan starts to pay.
- The deductible works the same way whether you have drug coverage through a prescription drug plan or an MA-PD plan.
- The full cost of the drug determines how much you will pay when the plan has a deductible. In other words, you pay the full cost for drugs subject to a deductible until the designated amount is met.
- A plan determines which medications are subject to its deductible. In many plans, that's Tiers 3, 4, and 5 drugs.
- The deductible applies to drugs the plan covers. If the plan does not cover a given medication, the beneficiary pays the full cost, and those payments will not apply to the deductible.
- It's possible to meet the deductible all at once, over time, or maybe never. Check out these examples.

Miguel takes a Tier 3 drug with a full cost of $1,038. He will meet the deductible in the first month.

Darlene's one medication, a Tier 4 muscle relaxant with a full cost of $21.26, is subject to the deductible. She will pay $21.26 every month and won't meet the plan's deductible this year.

Ray's regimen of seven drugs includes two Tier 3 medications in the mix. The full cost for those two is $70.96. He will meet the deductible in July.

- After meeting the deductible and entering the Initial Coverage payment stage, the plan can charge copayments or coinsurance. In many cases, costs can drop.
- Information in the Medicare Plan Finder (noted as retail costs) or the plan's benefit summary and EOB identifies the deductible amount and the tier for each medication.

Facts about the Donut Hole (Coverage Gap)

- In 2016 (the latest year for these data), over 5 million beneficiaries hit the donut hole.
- Generally, taking three or four brand-name drugs will land you in the donut hole. In some cases, one or two drugs advertised on television could do it.

The recommended dose of one biologic to treat ankylosing spondylitis has a full cost of about $5,500 in the Milwaukee area. A person taking that medication will likely pass through the first three stages, including the donut hole, right into Catastrophic Coverage in the first month or two of drug coverage.

- Those who reach the donut hole will likely do so year after year. That's because they take medications to treat chronic conditions, those that cannot be cured.
- About 3.7 million Part D plan members reached Catastrophic Coverage in 2020.

Prescription Medications That a Plan Does Not Cover

Here's a situation that could happen to you.

Khandi's physician ordered a new medication to treat a long-standing medical problem. She discovered her Part D plan didn't cover this drug. She thought drug plans were supposed to cover any medication.

This is not a rare event. Yet many are surprised to discover that an essential drug is not covered by their Part D plan. Unfortunately, you can't check a list of all noncovered drugs because there isn't one. Instead, CMS has rules about what drugs plans can and can't cover, and then plans put together their formularies (lists of covered medications).

Let's start with the categories of drugs that Part D plans cannot cover.

1. CMS's list of noncovered drugs.
   - drugs to treat anorexia, weight loss, weight gain, cold or cough symptoms, erectile dysfunction, or fertility problems,
   - drugs for cosmetic purposes or hair growth,
   - prescription vitamins and minerals, and
   - over-the-counter drugs (purchased without a prescription).
2. Drugs that are not approved by the Food and Drug Administration (FDA), such as desiccated thyroid or lidocaine.
3. Those drugs that Part A, hospital insurance, and Part B, medical insurance, cover, such as chemotherapy and vaccinations. (See chap. 6, "Part B, Medical Insurance.")

Then CMS has a list of protected drug classes, groups of drugs that have similar effects on the body or treat the same symptoms. Plans must cover every medication in these classes:

- immunosuppressants (to prevent the rejection of organ transplants),
- antiretrovirals (to control HIV/AIDS),

- antidepressants,
- antipsychotics,
- anticonvulsants (to treat seizures), and
- antineoplastics (to treat cancer).

Finally, there are drugs a plan chooses to cover. In all other nonprotected classes, a plan must cover at least two drugs. Beta-blockers are one of the many other classes of drugs. In this category, a plan might cover atenolol and metoprolol but not propranolol.

The actions you can take if a drug isn't covered depend on the drug.

- A plan will not approve a drug that's on the list of those that no plan can cover unless you get a medically necessary exception (not easy to do).
- For drugs a plan chooses not to cover, you have options.
  - If a brand-name medication is not covered, ask your doctor about a generic equivalent.
  - Find out whether there are any other prescription drugs in your plan's formulary that would be effective.
  - Your physician can submit a formulary exception, a request to obtain a Part D drug that is not included on a plan sponsor's formulary. Each plan has a procedure, but the physician's statement must prove that the noncovered drug is necessary to treat the medical condition and no alternatives on the formulary would work. A plan will grant medically necessary exemptions. If the plan denies the request, there is an appeals process.
  - You could pay for it yourself.
- Finally, during the Open Enrollment Period (OEP), October 15–December 7, check out the plans available to you. You probably will find one that works.

- There is always the option to purchase noncovered medications outside of the prescription drug plan with a coupon or discount card. (See chap. 6, "Questions and Answers about Part D Drug Coverage.")

Part D Vaccinations

You learned in chapter 6, "Part B, Medical Insurance," that Part B covers many vaccines, such as those for the flu, pneumonia, and COVID, to name a few. Part D covers just about every other vaccine. These include the following:

- shingles (known as Shingrix),
- hepatitis B administered to non-high-risk individuals, and
- DTaP (diphtheria, tetanus, pertussis).

The applicable cost sharing will apply, including the plan's deductible and copayment or coinsurance.

Getting Part D vaccinations in a physician's office can create problems, no matter the Medicare path you chose. To avoid issues, visit a pharmacy that is in the drug plan's network. Many pharmacies will allow you to schedule an appointment for your vaccinations.

Seven Tips for Medication Safety

As a home care nurse for many years, medication safety was a big concern. I had to check all drugs a patient was taking to help prevent adverse drug events (harm from a drug) or medication errors. According to Health.gov, such errors account for more than 3.5 million physician office visits and one million emergency department visits each year, with a cost of almost $21 billion.

If you take medications, here are some tips to help prevent medication mistakes.

- Keep your list of drugs and allergies up to date.
  - Carry the list on you.
  - Share it with physicians, even those who did not prescribe any drugs. This helps prevent complications—like taking two drugs, ordered by different doctors, to treat the same problem.
- Follow up with blood tests a doctor orders. These tests monitor the therapeutic effectiveness of the drugs and determine the impact on vital organs, such as the kidneys.
- Know about your drugs—when and how to take them, what they treat, any interactions with food or other drugs, side effects, and when to call your physician.
- Take the right dose of the right medication at the right time in the right way.
  - Start by reading the labels and following instructions. If the label says to take with food or on an empty stomach, do that. If the drug is ordered for seven days, take it for seven, even if you're feeling better after a couple doses.
  - Know what to do if you miss a dose. You can take some drugs as soon as you realize your mistake, but with others, you must wait to take them on schedule.
- Don't take another person's medications or share yours.
- Report side effects and interactions to your doctor.
- Keep drugs safe.
  - Store them in the original containers where they cannot be reached by others who shouldn't, such as grandchildren.
  - Know that heat, moisture, air, and light can damage drugs.
  - Ask your pharmacist about any safety or storage concerns.

Remember to Take Your Medications

Taking medications as directed was likely the biggest problem I saw as a home health nurse. Patients forgot to take their pills, lost track of when to take them, or couldn't remember whether they took them.

Even I have had this problem. I take blood pressure pills twice a day. Too many times I had to ask myself, Did you take your pills this morning or last night? I solved this problem with two inexpensive weekly pill organizers: morning pills in one, evening pills in the second.

There are many other ways to track administration, ranging from a simple chart or checklist all the way to more expensive pill dispensers. Do what it takes to make sure you take your medications on time.

Questions and Answers about Part D Drug Coverage

If the donut hole closed, how come drugs aren't free?

In the early days of Part D drug plans, those who landed in the donut hole had to pay 100 percent of the cost for every drug. (That's why this is officially known as the Coverage Gap. Insurance companies didn't cover the drugs.) Some beneficiaries could not afford this, so they quit taking their medications.

Then the ACA provided discounts. In 2012, the discount for brand-name drugs was 50 percent, and for generics, it was 14 percent. Every year since, discounts gradually increased until the donut hole closed completely in 2020.

The closing of the donut hole simply means everyone will pay a straight 25 percent of the cost of medications in the Coverage Gap, the same as in Initial Coverage. The biggest difference is how you'll pay that 25 percent. In Initial

Coverage, you pay a flat rate; in the Coverage Gap, you pay 25 percent. For many, this will cause sticker shock, as with this situation.

> Martin takes three medications, two Tier 1 and one Tier 3. In Initial Coverage, he pays $2 for Tier 1 and $47 for Tier 3.
> In the Coverage Gap, he will pay a straight 25 percent of the drugs' cost. His Tier 1 medications will drop to $0.79 and $0.94, but his Tier 3 medication will explode to $562 (25 percent of $2,161).

How does mail order work?

Those who have Part D coverage have an option to get 90-day supplies of prescribed medications through mail order, delivered to the home. In many plans, this can be a cost-effective option. Each insurer has its own mail-order program, so discuss with a plan representative how to set up the service.

Also consider the Part D Mail Order Auto-Ship program. Your plan can ship refills of drugs that you have been on for at least four consecutive months automatically to your home. You won't have to contact the plan or have the plan contact you every time a refill is due.

Can I get a 90-day refill of my medications from pharmacies?

Some retail pharmacies may also offer a 60- or 90-day supply of covered prescription drugs. Check with your plan about pharmacies that can do this.

Will my Part D drug plan cover compounded drugs?

According to the FDA, drug compounding is a process of combining, mixing, or altering ingredients to create a medication tailored to the needs of an individual patient and includes the combining of two or more drugs.

There are important reasons that doctors prescribe compounded drugs, such as if there is no uncompounded version available or the patient has unique needs. However, the FDA does not approve compounded drugs, so Part D plans could not cover them. Part D also does not cover bulk powder, used in most of these drugs.

There are some situations in which a drug can qualify for Part D reimbursement. In simplest terms, the drug must include at least one FDA-approved drug component; it is prescribed for a medically indicated reason and, generally, includes a drug on the plan's formulary.

To answer the question, maybe the drug plan will cover a compounded drug, or maybe it won't. This is a very complicated subject, so discuss your concerns with a pharmacist, either yours or one with your plan.

Does it matter whether a plan charges a copayment or a coinsurance for a drug?

A copayment is a specific dollar amount that the plan sets for a drug. That is what you would pay for any refills in a calendar year.

With a coinsurance, you pay a percentage of the cost. Here's an example.

> A drug has a retail cost of $100. One plan charges a $42 copayment; the second, a 33 percent coinsurance, which would be $33.

Know that with a coinsurance, if the cost of the drug increases during the year, you will pay more.

Why do you say that getting Part D vaccinations in a physician's office can be problematic?

The problem is a doctor's office is not a pharmacy. It is not in a plan's network and has not negotiated any prices. For

Part D to cover the medication, a doctor's office must either be able to:

- coordinate with an in-network pharmacy to bill the vaccine, or
- bill the plan electronically for the vaccine.

If the physician's office can't do either, you would have to pay the full cost up front for the vaccine plus the fees associated with administration. You could then submit a paper claim to the drug plan for reimbursement of the plan's share. (You would be responsible for the plan's cost sharing.) It's possible that the physician's cost for the vaccination might be more than the plan's approved amount, which would be money out of your pocket.

Your best option for Part D vaccinations will be to go to an in-network pharmacy. This may not be as convenient, but it will certainly be more cost-effective.

Remember, you can receive Part B vaccinations, like the flu shot, in a physician's office.

How does my Medicare Advantage plan's over-the-counter (OTC) medication benefit work?

Some plans offer a benefit that allows members to purchase non-prescription health items. Check the plan's information to answer these questions.

- What OTC medications can you purchase? Many plans will cover cold, flu, digestion, pain, and sleep medications, along with denture-related products and first aid supplies.
- How much can you purchase? Plans generally have limits, such as $100 every quarter.

- Where can you get OTC medications? You may have to use a network pharmacy, but some plans will deliver to your home.
- Will you get a drug card, or must you submit receipts? That depends on the plan. Know the procedure and keep records.

Can I use a $25 coupon to help pay for a very expensive medication?

Manufacturers issue coupons to lure consumers into purchasing a particular coffee or cereal. However, for those with Medicare, things change.

A coupon can entice a Medicare beneficiary to purchase medication A instead of medication B. If the products involved are part of a federal program, such as Part D medications, the anti-kickback statute comes into play. This statute makes "it a criminal offense to knowingly and willfully offer, pay, solicit, or receive any remuneration to induce or reward the referral or generation of business reimbursable by any federal health care program." In other words, using a coupon to purchase a Part D medication would constitute a fraudulent claim under federal law.

This same stipulation applies to drug discount programs. The beneficiary pays a fee and gets discounts on selected medications.

You always have the option to purchase medications outside of the Part D prescription drug plan. If there is a valuable coupon or discount, tell the pharmacist that you want to pay for this drug and not to process it through the insurance.

There may be other times that you opt to pay out-of-pocket for a medication. Up until 2018, pharmacists were bound by a "gag clause." They could not inform beneficiaries that the plan copayment, such as $47, was more than the out-of-pocket cost for a particular drug, $25.

Now Part D drug plans can no longer enforce gag clauses, and you can learn about cost-saving opportunities. Address any concerns with your pharmacist.

Living with Your Medicare Path

So far throughout this book, you've learned the basics about Medicare hospital, medical, and drug coverage and fine points that apply to the Original Medicare and Medicare Advantage Paths. It's time to pull together a list of important considerations to remember as you move forward with Medicare.

The Original Medicare Path

- Along with Part A and Part B, you will have a Medigap policy and Part D drug plan.
- This is a "pay-now" approach. You pay monthly premiums, and then you will have predictable out-of-pocket costs.
- You'll be able to change your drug plan every year during the OEP.
- However, making changes in your Medigap policy will depend on your health, your state of residence, and whether you have a guaranteed issue right.
- If you want dental and vision coverage, you can enroll in stand-alone plans.
- Figure out how you'll pay for items Medicare does not cover, like long-term care.

The Medicare Advantage Path

- You can get a plan that includes prescription drug coverage and benefits that Medicare does not cover, such as dental and vision services, hearing aids, transportation, personal aid, and more. Check the criteria and limits.
- Plans are network-based.

- You may need referrals to see doctors other than your primary.
- Prior authorization is a fact of life.
- Medicare Advantage is "pay as you go." Plans have no or very low monthly premiums, but you can pay deductibles, copayments, and coinsurance until you reach the plan's maximum out-of-pocket limit.
- Pay attention to that maximum limit. If you become ill or have an accident, the medical costs you pay may reach that amount.
- You have an annual opportunity to change plans.
- Your ability to change to the Original Medicare Path and get a Medigap policy depends on whether you have a guaranteed issue right.

Questions and Answers about Your Medicare Path

What should I do if I get a denial letter?

Part A or Part B or a Medicare Advantage plan can issue a denial and refuse to pay if a medical treatment or service does not meet the specified coverage criteria. Denials happen for many reasons, but one of the most common is that the claim does not support medical necessity, meaning it wasn't necessary to treat a medical condition. Medicare Advantage denials can also happen if the plans rules are not followed.

When there's a denial, Medicare or the Medicare Advantage plan sends a notice explaining what happened, the implications, your right to appeal, and how to submit one.

A recent *Health Affairs* study reported that Medicare Part A and Part B and Medicare Advantage plans issued more than 5.6 million claim denials between 2014 and 2019, totaling $416 million in noncovered claims. The Office of Inspector General (OIG) found that only 2.6 percent of Part A and Part B denials and 1 percent of Medicare Advantage denials are appealed. However, as the OIG reported, 51 percent of Part B denials and 75 percent of Medicare Advantage denials were overturned. That can imply the denials were inappropriate.

Many beneficiaries probably believe an appeal is not worth the effort or have no idea where to start. But there are resources to help. For instance, the Medicare Interactive website, a reference tool powered by the Medicare Rights Center, has a page dedicated to appeal basics. Find that at www.medicare -links.com/medicare-interactive-appeal-basics. Or check out the information on Medicare.gov at www.medicare-links.com/ file-a-medicare-appeal.

If Medicare won't pay for a necessary procedure, can I get reimbursement from a Medicare Advantage plan or Medigap policy?

A Medigap policy only pays its share of services that Medicare covers, so you cannot get reimbursement if Medicare didn't pay.

The same rules apply to Medicare Advantage plans. However, some plans can choose to cover things Medicare doesn't, such as physical examinations or glasses. All that depends on the plan, so check the EOC.

What should I know about the maximum out-of-pocket limit for Medicare Advantage plans?

You will likely have a no- or low-premium plan. But there are costs, and that's why there's a maximum limit.

- Once you reach that limit, the plan covers any costs for the remainder of the year.
- This limit excludes monthly premiums and prescription medications.
- Services not usually covered by Medicare, such as hearing or vision, are not counted in the limit.

- The maximum limit, established by Medicare, is $7,550 for in-network services.
- If you are in a plan that covers services you receive from out-of-network providers, such as a PPO, your plan will set two annual limits on your out-of-pocket costs. One limit is for in-network costs, a $7,550 maximum, and the other is for combined in-network and out-of-network costs, with a maximum of $11,300.
- Each plan determines its maximum out-of-pocket limit and can opt to offer a lower limit. On the West Coast, the limits are low, some under $1,000. As you move east, limits tend to increase. In 2021, according to the Kaiser Family Foundation, the weighted average out-of-pocket limit was $5,091 for in-network services and $9,208 for in-network and out-of-network services combined.

What can I do if my physician drops out of the Medicare Advantage network during the year?

The plan must notify you if your physician leaves or is dropped from the network and can often help you find a new doctor.

CMS may deem the change in network to be "significant," based on the number of members affected, the size of the service area, and the timing, among other things. Those affected by a significant change get a special enrollment period to join a new plan during the year.

In some cases, you may just have to accept the changes until you can find a different plan during one of the OEPs that has your physician in-network. (See chap. 8, "Open Enrollment Period [OEP].")

If my physician submits the prior authorization forms, is there anything I should know?

As you may have noticed, Medicare Advantage plans can require prior authorization on just about any service. Here is what you should know.

- Check the plan's EOC to identify services and procedures that require prior authorization.
- Find a copy of your insurance company's form or process. Check the website or call a plan representative. Your physician may need it, and you'll know exactly what must be included.
- Confirm that whoever in your physician's office is in charge of this process knows that you need an authorization and the date due.
- Double-check that documentation is submitted and that approval is received before the procedure. You may want to confirm your costs.
- Remember, if you move forward without authorization, you may be responsible for the full cost.
- Appeal a denial, following the company's process.

Many retirees establish a budget to manage finances. Now that you'll be living with Medicare, the next chapter gets into how much everything will cost. Warning: It may be more than you expect.

Chapter 7

Medicare Premiums

If you believe Medicare is free, you're in for a big shock. You've already been exposed to the cost sharing you can face with Part A, Part B, Medigap policies, Part D drug plans, and Medicare Advantage plans. Now you'll learn about the premiums—the ones you expect and one you don't, IRMAA (the income-related monthly adjustment amount).

Medicare costs change every year. Find the current ones at www.dianeomdahl.com/updates.

Premiums for Medicare Coverage

Part A, Hospital Insurance, and Part B, Medical Insurance

Here is what you need to know about premiums for hospital and medical insurance.

- Medicare Part A is premium-free for those who have earned 40 credits (paid Medicare taxes for 10 years) or whose current or former spouse has.
- However, those who do not have all the credits can purchase Part A. If they have earned 30 credits, the monthly premium in 2022 was $274, and those with less than 30 pay $499.
- The standard premium for Part B was $170.10 in 2022.
- Higher-income beneficiaries will pay more, based on their income. (See chap. 7, "IRMAA.")

How to pay these premiums depends on your situation.

- For those who receive retirement benefits from Social Security, the Railroad Retirement Board, or Civil Service, the Part B premium will be deducted automatically from the benefit payment. (Those who pay for Part A do not yet qualify for Social Security benefits.)
- If you're not receiving benefits, there are three common ways to pay the bills.
    1. Sign up for Medicare Easy Pay. (See chap. 7, "Questions and Answers about Medicare Premiums.")
    2. Mail a check or your credit card information for premium payments to the address noted on the invoice.
    3. Pay the invoice through your MyMedicare.gov account.

Additional Coverage

The insurance company sponsoring the Part D drug or Medicare Advantage plan determines the monthly premium. These beneficiaries can:

- arrange payment with the insurer, which means paying each invoice or setting up autopayments; or
- have the premiums deducted from their monthly retirement benefit payment, just as with Part B.

The premiums for Medigap policies (Medicare supplement plans) cannot be deducted from monthly retirement benefits. Those who have this coverage can either pay the invoices or make payment arrangements with the insurer. A convenient way is monthly deductions from a checking or savings account.

IRMAA

Here's a surprise that happens to many Medicare beneficiaries.

> I received a letter from Social Security saying that I must pay more for Medicare Part B.

You just met IRMAA, the income-related monthly adjustment amount. (This is not the hurricane—it has two As. But if you don't know how to handle this issue, it could be a financial tempest.) Since 2007, higher-income beneficiaries have had to pay additional premiums for Part B, medical insurance, and since 2011, they also pay more for Part D, prescription drug coverage.

The Basics

Social Security determines who will pay IRMAA based on the IRS tax return two years prior to the current year. For those enrolling in Medicare Part B in 2022, Social Security reviewed their 2020 tax records. (In some situations, Social Security will use three-year-old data or base decisions on tax information provided by the beneficiaries.)

2020 Adjusted Gross Income + Tax-exempt Interest Income		2022 IRMAA	
Single Filers	**Individuals Filing Jointly**	PART B	PART D
≤$91,000	≤$182,000	$0.00	$0.00
>$91,000 to ≤$114,000	>$182,000 to ≤$228,000	$68.00	$12.40
>$114,000 to ≤$142,000	>$228,000 to ≤$284,000	$170.10	$32.10
>$142,000 to ≤$170,000	>$284,000 to ≤$340,000	$272.20	$51.70
>$170,000 to <$500,000	>$340,000 to <$750,000	$374.20	$71.30
≥$500,000	≥$750,000	$408.20	$77.90
Married Individuals Filing Separately	PART B	PART D	
≤$91,000	$0.00	$0.00	
>$91,000 to <$409,000	$374.20	$71.30	
≤$409,000	$408.20	$77.90	

Then every November, Social Security will look at the next tax record to determine whether IRMAA will apply in the new year, as in this situation.

> Diana turned 65 in January 2022. Social Security reviewed her 2020 income tax return to make the initial IRMAA determination. In November 2022, Social Security reviewed her 2021 tax record to see whether she will be subject to IRMAA in 2023.

Two data elements on a tax return, adjusted gross income and tax-exempt interest income, determine the modified adjusted gross income (MAGI) for IRMAA determinations. If the total crosses the threshold, IRMAA applies. In 2022, the thresholds were as follows:

- $182,000 for a married individual filing a joint return (both spouses will have to pay any adjustments),
- $91,000 for a single filer, and
- $91,000 for a married individual filing a separate return.

After crossing the threshold, there are five levels or tiers of payments. (See chart earlier in this chapter.)

Social Security will send written notices to beneficiaries subject to IRMAA. These notices explain that IRMAA will apply, the information used to compute the MAGI, what the beneficiary can do if the tax information is wrong, how to deal with a life-changing event (LCE), how to contact Social Security if there are concerns about the information used, and appeal rights.

An LCE

Many new Medicare beneficiaries get the IRMAA notices. Two years ago, they had good-paying positions, but now with retirement, their income will drop substantially. When it looks at the tax return for the current year, Social Security would see that there is a drop in income; however, there are no automatic changes to IRMAA. The drop could be due to bad investments or a gambling habit.

That's when knowledge of LCEs is important. Social Security has identified eight LCEs that can cause a significant drop in income and justify a reduction or suspension of the higher premium. These include:

- death of a spouse,
- marriage,
- divorce or annulment,
- work reduction,
- work stoppage (retirement or termination),
- loss of income-producing property (beyond the individual's control),
- loss or reduction of pension income (plan failure or termination or scheduled cessation), and
- employer settlement payment (as a result of an employer or former employer's closure, bankruptcy, or reorganization).

The last seven can apply to the beneficiary or spouse. For instance, a spouse's retirement, even if not yet on Medicare, can affect the family income.

When one of these events reduces income significantly, the beneficiary can file a notice with Social Security, asking for a new determination and a reduction in IRMAA. The form, Medicare Income-Related Monthly Adjustment Amount—Life-Changing Event (SSA-44), notifies Social Security that the circumstances have changed. Find it at www .medicare-links.com/life-changing-event-form.

If your income will drop at least one tier because of the LCE, file the SSA-44 as soon as possible after receiving the notification.

- Follow the instructions on the form.
- Note your best guess for income after the LCE.

- Include documentation to support the LCE. For example, Social Security will accept an employment termination letter, a death certificate, or a divorce decree.
- Submit the documentation and form to the address noted in Social Security's initial determination letter.

Once Social Security has determined that you meet the qualifying criteria, you'll see a reduction in premiums. But know that Social Security will confirm your guesstimated income after you have filed the tax return for the year and then make any necessary adjustments. For instance, if your income was lower than you estimated and as a result you paid more than you should have, Social Security will issue a refund.

If Social Security does not reduce the adjustments after requesting a new initial determination, you have the right to file an appeal by completing a Request for Reconsideration (SSA-561-U2). Download the form at www.medicare-links.com/request-for-reconsideration-form.

One-Time Income

Other one-time-only income—such as capital gains, IRA withdrawals, or conversion from a traditional IRA to a Roth IRA—may put you over the threshold. One-time income will affect your Medicare premiums for only one year. In the absence of an LCE, there is nothing you can do to reduce what you must pay. A financial advisor can help you make smart financial decisions.

Questions and Answers about Medicare Premiums

What is included in the Part B or Part D premiums I pay?

The four possible costs that make up Part B bills include:

- the standard Part B premium, $170.10 in 2022,
- Part B adjustments (additional amounts) based on your income, if you're subject to IRMAA, and
- the monthly Part B late enrollment penalty if you missed your chance to enroll.

The Part D premium components are:

- the premium for your stand-alone Part D drug plan,
- Part D IRMAA, if applicable, and
- the monthly late enrollment penalty if you did not have creditable drug coverage for more than two months.

How do I get billed for the Part B premium and IRMAA?

If you are not receiving Social Security benefits, somewhere around the 10th day of the month, you'll get a Medicare Premium Bill (CMS-500) that includes the standard premiums for Part A and Part B, and IRMAA for Part B and/or Part D. Depending on your situation, the invoices will come monthly or quarterly. Bills for new beneficiaries can include more months until they get into the billing cycle.

If you are already receiving retirement benefits, the premiums will come out of your benefit amount. Social Security's annual notice that you get before the new year will identify the amount you'll pay. If the monthly benefit is not enough to cover the entire bill, the Centers for Medicare and Medicaid Services (CMS) sends an invoice. It never deducts a partial premium payment from your retirement benefit.

Medicare bills contain quite a bit of information. Learn how to read one at www.medicare-links.com/medicare-premium -bill. (The sample is a delinquent bill, one you should never receive if you pay attention.)

What happens if I miss paying a premium?

If Medicare doesn't get the full payment for Part A (for those who must pay the premium), Part B (premium and IRMAA), or Part D IRMAA by the date noted on the bill, the next bill will show that the payment is late. You should send in the complete payment by the due date in that notice. If you don't meet that deadline and the payment is 90 days late, you'll get a final, delinquent bill. Pay that by the due date, or you'll get a termination letter that you lost your Medicare coverage. The letter will explain how to get your coverage back.

If you miss a payment for your drug or Medicare Advantage plan, the procedure depends on the individual plan. All plans must have a grace period of at least two months, and some have longer periods. Check the plan information for more details.

If you have a Medigap policy, ask the insurance company about how to handle missed payments. But the best case is not to miss payments. Policies purchased since 1992 are considered "guaranteed renewable." The insurer cannot drop a policyholder who pays premiums on time. If the policy is canceled for nonpayment, it's likely the individual will have to pass medical underwriting to get another policy.

> Don't risk cancelation of your Medicare coverage. Set up automatic payments.

How do I set up a Medicare Easy Pay account?

This is a free service that automatically deducts Medicare premium payments from a savings or checking account each month. The easiest way to establish an account is through your MyMedicare.gov account. Once logged in, select "My Premiums" and then "Sign Up" to complete a short online form. It may take up to two months for the automatic deductions to begin, so pay the invoices until then.

Check out "Understanding Your Medicare Easy Pay Premium Statement (CMS-20143)" at www.medicare-links.com/medicare-easy-pay-statement.

What is the Part B premium reduction?

This is more commonly known as the Medicare giveback benefit. You can qualify for this if there's a Medicare Advantage plan in your zip code that offers this benefit. (See chap. 3, "Making Your Medicare Path Decision.")

What is the hold harmless provision?

This special provision protects Social Security benefit payments from decreasing if there is a significant increase in the Part B premium. In simplest terms, the hold harmless provision kicks in when an increase in the annual Part B premium is greater than the Social Security cost-of-living adjustment (COLA). It limits the Part B premium to no more than the COLA. Here is how it works: The hold harmless provision would apply if the COLA increase for a beneficiary is $6 but the Part B premium goes up $9. The hold harmless provision does not apply to those who:

- enroll in Part B for the first time (the first year of enrollment),
- are subject to IRMAA, or
- are dually eligible (eligible for both Medicare and Medicaid) and Medicaid pays the Part B premium.

Can you explain the difference between an Explanation of Benefits (EOB) and a Medicare Summary Notice (MSN)?

An EOB is a notice, not a bill, that Medicare Advantage and Part D drug plans and Medigap policies send after you receive any medical services, supplies, or medications.

- The Medicare Advantage EOB is a summary of what you received, how much the provider billed, and how much you may owe or have paid.

- The drug plan EOB will identify the medications you received, how much you paid, and which drug payment stage you are in at that time. Medicare Advantage plans that include drug coverage will list this same information in an EOB.
- Medigap policies also send EOBs including additional information—how much Medicare paid and where you stand with meeting the Part B deductible.
- Each plan has its own format and layout for the EOB.
- Plans usually mail EOBs every month, and you may have the option to access it online through your account.

An MSN is not a bill and is sent to those who chose the Original Medicare Path.

- You will get an MSN for a three-month period if you received any services or supplies during that time. If you didn't get any services, you won't get a notice.
- The MSN shows the services or supplies that were billed to Medicare on your behalf; what Medicare Part A, hospital insurance, and Part B, medical insurance, paid; and how much you may owe the provider.
- The amount you owe does not consider what a Medigap policy may pay.
- Those who have the Original Medicare Path should prepare to receive an MSN from Medicare, an EOB from the Medigap policy and drug plan, and a bill from the provider.

If you see in an MSN or EOB that a service or item was not covered, check the comments or footnotes for an explanation.

Do not pay whatever these notices say you may owe. Wait until you receive the provider's bill, and then compare the coverage and costs. The provider bill should note what insurance has paid.

What income determines the MAGI for IRMAA?

The MAGI can include, as applicable, wages, capital gains, taxable interest, tax dividends, annuity income, business income, IRA distributions, and tax-exempt interest.

If I have a Medicare Advantage plan, do I pay IRMAA?

You must be enrolled in Part B to get a Medicare Advantage plan, so you will pay Part B IRMAA. If your plan includes prescription drug coverage, you will also pay Part D IRMAA.

Can I file an LCE for the sale of my house that puts me over the threshold?

Having to sell your home before moving into a retirement center may be life-changing for you, but it is not recognized as an LCE for a reduction in IRMAA. Unfortunately, you will likely have to pay IRMAA for one year.

If it is because of my income that we are over the IRMAA thresholds, does my spouse still have to pay?

Unfortunately, if you are married individuals filing a joint return, IRMAA applies to both of you.

However, if you think you would save money as married individuals filing separately, think again. Look at the IRMAA chart. (See chap. 7, "IRMAA.") You'll quickly realize that Medicare doesn't give these individuals a break when it comes to IRMAA.

Is it worth it for me to hire a financial advisor or a CPA who understands IRMAA?

The answer is a definite yes. Consider consulting with an advisor three or four years before you plan to enroll in Medicare. There may be things that can be done to reduce income that would be subject to IRMAA.

Once enrolled in Medicare, an advisor can also help manage the amount you may have to pay so you don't face a nasty surprise, like this couple did.

> Jeff and Ann had to withdraw money from an IRA. They were not aware of IRMAA, and they were shocked to get the notice of how much they would both pay. Then they got upset. In 2022, they reported an income of $194,000 and just "dribbled" over the threshold. They both had to pay an additional $80 every month.

You are in the home stretch of your journey to master Medicare. Take a moment to think about all you've learned. There are just a few more important topics in the final chapter.

Chapter 8

Other Important Things You Need to Know

There is no doubt that Medicare has a steep learning curve. You have to learn so many important concepts in a relatively short period of time. Then, just when you think you've covered everything, you turn the page to find more topics you need to know.

Open Enrollment and Changing Plans

Earlier in this book, you learned the importance of choosing the right path. Unless you live in Connecticut, Maine, Massachusetts, or New York, you may not be able to qualify for a Medigap policy if you decide to drop a Medicare Advantage plan.

However, you will have several opportunities to change your Part D drug or Medicare Advantage plan.

Open Enrollment Period (OEP)
The Open Enrollment Period (OEP), also known as the Annual Election Period, is an important time for those who have a stand-alone Part D drug plan or Medicare Advantage plan. It is your chance to see what your current coverage will look like next year and make any changes. The OEP runs from October 15 to December 7.

How important is reviewing coverage every year? A Kaiser Family Foundation study found that more than half of

Medicare beneficiaries do not review or compare their options annually. And it's likely these people will overpay for coverage. Another recent study discovered that over 90 percent of Medicare beneficiaries were not in the most cost-effective plan for their drug regimens.

Here are some recent examples that show how easy it is to overpay for your medications if you don't review your coverage.

> Rosanna takes an estrogen medication. Each year, it seems she is paying more for this drug. She was very surprised to find the copayment in plans in her area ranged from $20 to $600. She thought all plans charged the same.

> Paula was not happy when she had to pay over $500 for her eczema cream this year. She discovered that the plan she has had since age 65 took this medication off its drug list over a year ago. If she had caught this change and switched plans, her copayment would have dropped to $4.

> Barry had one of the cheapest drug plans for years and saw no reason to change. Last year, his premium was $26.40. Imagine his surprise when he got his January invoice and saw that his premium was $55. Barry wouldn't have been surprised if he had paid attention. Now, he is stuck paying a higher premium and cannot make changes until the next OEP.

These three individuals were just going with the flow, thinking everything would be fine. However, that attitude can lead to problems, as they discovered. From now on, they won't ignore the chance to evaluate their coverage.

And then there can be issues with the Medicare Advantage Path, such as with these two situations.

In July, Curtis was notified that his physician was no longer in his plan's network.

Sandy was shocked to learn that the out-of-pocket maximum for her plan will increase by over $1,500 next year.

They need to consider making changes when they can, or they will run into problems.

Here's what to do during Open Enrollment.

1. *Open the Annual Notice of Changes.*
   By law, sponsors of Medicare Advantage or Part D drug plans must send this notice to all plan members at least 15 days before the start of Open Enrollment, usually in late September. It outlines changes in the plan's benefits, coverage, formulary, premium, and/or costs that will take effect January 1.
2. *Check for any of these changes in your drug coverage for the next year.*
   Here are some of the things that can change.
   - The plan's formulary: If it changes, one or more of your drugs may not be covered.
   - Tier of drug: An increase, such as from Tier 2 to Tier 3, will likely cost you more.
   - Premium, deductible, and cost sharing: Determine whether you will pay more for your medications.
   - Pharmacies: A change in status of your favorite pharmacy from a preferred to a standard or out-of-network one can really cost money.
3. *Check out changes in the medical coverage if you have a Medicare Advantage plan.*
   - Are your physicians still in-network?
   - What are the premium and health plan deductibles?
   - What is the plan's out-of-pocket limit?

- Are the benefits you're using still available and the best option? For instance, dental coverage limits could be slashed. Maybe you need hearing aids next year.

4. *Evaluate other plans that are available.*
   Even if you're completely satisfied with your current plan, check out what might be available through the Medicare Plan Finder.

5. *Decide what you want to do.*
   - If your current plan is still the best, sit tight. The plan will renew automatically on January 1.
   - If you determine the plan won't work, enroll in a new one by December 7. You can call a customer service number or do this online through the plan's website. (The closer you get to the December 7 deadline, the more challenging phone enrollment may be.) Once you've enrolled, you will be automatically disenrolled (dropped) from your existing plan as of the new year, and the new plan will begin January 1.

Besides reviewing plans, there are a few other things you can do during this OEP.

- Drop Medicare Advantage and return to Original Medicare, Part A and Part B, and get a drug plan. Your ability to purchase a Medigap policy, however, will depend on whether you have a guaranteed issue right.
- Change from Original Medicare to a Medicare Advantage plan.
- Join a Part D drug plan. Know that if you did not have creditable drug coverage from another source, you can face a late enrollment penalty.
- Drop your Medicare drug coverage completely.

Pay Attention and Open Your Mail

If you're like me, you open your mailbox and find it stuffed with junk mail. Walking into the house, you flip through it and then probably toss most of it in the recycling bin. Now that you're on Medicare, it's time to change your habits. Start opening and reading any mail that comes from Medicare, your Medicare Advantage or Part D drug plan, or your Medigap policy. Here are three compelling reasons.

- There can be changes during the year in your prescription drug coverage. The plan may drop a brand-name drug if a generic alternative becomes available. Plans can change or add coverage rules for specific medications.
- There can be significant changes in a Medicare Advantage plan's network. Hospitals, doctors, and other providers can come and go from a plan's network anytime during the year.
- There can be changes in your costs or coverage of services.

When there are changes like these, the plan will send a notice explaining what happened and your options. If you don't open the mail, you won't know what's happening, and that could create problems.

You will also receive information from the insurance companies about the services and medications you received. (See chap. 7, "Questions and Answers about Medicare Premiums.")

Medicare Advantage OEP

This OEP goes from January 1 to March 31 every year. It is only for those who are enrolled in a Medicare Advantage plan. During this period, you can:

- switch from a Medicare Advantage plan, with or without drug coverage, to another Medicare Advantage plan, with or without drug coverage; or
- drop your Medicare Advantage plan, return to Original Medicare, and enroll in a stand-alone Part D drug plan. As noted in chapter 3, "Changing Paths down the Road," you may need a guaranteed issue right to get a Medigap policy.

Once you have made your change, the new coverage will begin the first of the next month.

5-Star Plan Special Enrollment Period (SEP)

A 5-star plan can provide higher-quality coverage and a more positive experience, along with better benefits. In 2022, there were 74 Medicare Advantage plans with drug coverage and 13 drug plans that received a 5-star rating. If one is available in your area, you have a special opportunity to enroll in that plan at any time between December 8 and November 30. Contact the 5-star plan to enroll.

PS: There is nothing that would prohibit you from enrolling in a 5-star plan during the fall OEP. The 5-star plan SEP just provides a special opportunity outside of that time.

State-Specific Opportunities

Some states have rules that provide residents with a guaranteed issue right to switch to a different Medigap policy.

- Five states—California, Idaho, Illinois, Nevada, and Oregon—have some version of a "birthday rule." You can switch to a different policy during a period related to your birthday.

- Missouri offers an annual opportunity to switch that's connected to the policy's anniversary date.
- Washington allows enrollees to change plans at any time of the year.
- Those living in Connecticut, Maine, Massachusetts, and New York can switch Medigap plans without having to pass medical underwriting. (See chap. 3, "Changing Paths down the Road.")

As you can see, these opportunities are all slightly different. If you live in one of these states, please check the state insurance website for complete details.

Medicare and Social Security Representatives

A power of attorney (POA) is a powerful thing. A financial POA document allows an appointed person to make financial, legal, and property decisions on another individual's behalf. A medical POA is a durable POA for health care. This allows an agent (a trusted friend or family member) to make important and necessary health care decisions if the individual becomes incapacitated or unable to communicate or participate in care.

It's important that you have POA documents that are updated as needed. However, as valuable as these documents are, they will not stand alone for Medicare or Social Security.

Medicare Personal Representative

Sometimes, in spite of our best efforts, life presents a situation that we may not be prepared to handle.

Doug, 77 years old, was hospitalized after suffering a stroke. He was unable to communicate. His wife, Debra, was trying to deal with some cost and coverage issues related to his care. She tried calling

Medicare but could not talk with anyone because she did not have authority to do so. She was baffled. Her husband had executed powers of attorney, so what was the problem?

Doug may have had POA documents, but he did not have a Medicare authorized representative. By law, Medicare requires a person's written permission to use or provide personal medical information for any purpose not defined in the privacy notice contained in the Medicare & You handbook. Doug had not given any permission.

You can avoid those problems by completing the following form: 1-800-MEDICARE Authorization to Disclose Personal Health Information. (Find the form at www.medicare-links.com/medicare-authorization-to-disclose.) This will give your representative the authority to talk with Medicare, research and choose Medicare coverage, handle claims, and even file an appeal.

Note these specific instructions for completion of the form.

- Check whether you authorize Medicare to release limited or any information. If limited, identify the type of information, such as claims, eligibility, or premiums.
- Identify whether the authorization applies for a specified period of time or indefinitely.
- Submit the form by mail to Medicare. There is no fax or email submission of the application.
- However, once you have a representative, you can update information at any time through your MyMedicare.gov account.
- You have the right to revoke this authorization at any time.

Medicare Plans Authorization

There's another authorization you'll need for Medicare, just in case. This will give your representative permission to deal with the individual Medicare coverage you may have, be it a Medicare Advantage or Part D prescription drug plan or a Medigap policy.

This form provides another person with the authority to speak to plan representatives about claims or coverage, update contact information, and more, depending on the individual plan.

Every plan has an authorization form, and it goes by many different names, such as authorization to share personal information or authorization to share protected health information. To start this process, check the plan's member information or contact a customer service representative.

Social Security Representative Payee

Doug and Debra encountered another issue. Just as with Medicare, POAs do not give the legal authority to negotiate and manage a beneficiary's Social Security payments or talk with Social Security about another person's benefits.

> After hospitalization and rehabilitation, Doug returned home to the care of his wife. His major lingering effect was expressive aphasia, the inability to speak or write.
>
> A few months later, Debra decided to change banks. She called Social Security to provide new account information for direct deposit of their monthly benefits. The agent noted her information but would not update Doug's account until someone from Social Security talked with him. Given his condition, that likely would not happen.

The agent introduced Debra to the Social Security representative payee.

- Social Security appoints a payee for anyone who can't manage his or her Social Security benefits.

- A representative payee can be a person or an organization.
- The payee receives the Social Security payments and is given the authority to use them on the beneficiary's behalf to pay for the current and future needs.
- The payee must know what the beneficiary needs in order to make wise decisions.
- A payee must also keep records of expenses.
- In most cases, a payee is not paid for carrying out these duties.

The first step in becoming a representative is to contact the local Social Security office to schedule an interview. Social Security will perform a thorough investigation and may conduct a home visit or financial record review. Once appointed, the representative payee must keep records of expenses and may have to account for the benefit payments received.

It's likely you don't need a representative payee now, but who knows about the future. Social Security allows advance designation for those who apply for or are already receiving retirement benefits. You can identify up to three trusted family members or friends who could serve as your representative payee in the future. If and when the time comes that you need someone to manage your benefits, Social Security will contact a person on your list.

You can submit your advance designation request when you apply for benefits or after you are already receiving benefits through your *my* Social Security account.

Fraud and Scams

A scam describes any fraudulent act or operation to cheat someone out of something, such as money or a Medicare or credit card number. The FBI estimates that seniors lose more than $3 billion every year to fraudsters. There is a scam where a caller says a grandchild is in grave trouble, and grandma must send money. Another caller promises free tests or supplies. All it takes is your Medicare number. One of the most lucrative scams targets lonely seniors, who in one year lost almost $84 million looking for romance. The list goes on and on.

These seven facts can help you avoid becoming a victim.

- Medicare and Social Security rarely call beneficiaries. If a call is necessary:
    - they don't ask for your Medicare or Social Security numbers because they already have them,
    - they will not request your bank account or credit card numbers,
    - they do not threaten to stop retirement or Medicare benefits, and
    - they will not demand immediate payment over the phone.
- Don't provide your Social Security or Medicare numbers or your bank account or credit card information to anyone calling you.
- Resist the pressure to take immediate action. Legitimate businesses give you time to make a decision.
- Never send gift cards or use a money transfer service to pay a caller.
- If you are unsure about what you heard in a phone call, contact Social Security ([800] 772-1213), Medicare ([800] 633-4227), or your bank or credit card company directly.
- Do not answer calls from unknown numbers. A real caller will leave a message. If you don't have caller ID, hang up once you realize the caller is not legitimate.
- And remember, if it sounds too good to be true, it is.

Long-Term Care (LTC)

You may wonder why long-term care (LTC) is in a book about Medicare. If you're healthy, you might think you'll never need it. However, consider these startling statistics.

- A person turning 65 today has almost a 70 percent chance of needing some type of LTC services and support in their remaining years.
- 20 percent of those turning 65 will need care for longer than five years.
- About 35 percent of people who reach age 65 are expected to enter a nursing home for LTC at least once in their lifetime.

Or maybe you're one of the 56 percent of middle-income Baby Boomers who believe Medicare will pay for their ongoing LTC. *Medicare does not now and never has covered LTC.*

LTC is in a Medicare book because most of us will need it and have to figure out how to pay for it. These facts can help clear away the confusion about LTC.

1. *LTC is a range of services and support to meet health or personal care needs over an extended period of time.* Often called custodial care, this is nonmedical care provided by nonlicensed caregivers.
2. *The aging process is the primary reason most will need LTC.* As we age, we can lose the ability to perform activities of daily living (ADL). The six essential ADL include the ability to independently eat, dress, walk or transfer from one position to another, bathe, use the toilet, and maintain bowel and bladder continence.

    Those with arthritis and similar chronic diseases or dementia, such as Alzheimer's disease, are also likely to need LTC.

3. *A variety of settings provide LTC.* These include:
   - an adult day-care center,
   - a nursing home,
   - an assisted-living facility or residential care community, and
   - the most common location, the home, with care provided by a family member or friend. In 2017, over 40 million caregivers provided the equivalent of $470 billion in unpaid assistance.
4. *LTC can be costly.* In 2019, the Congressional Research Service reported that the United States spent an estimated $426.1 billion on LTC services.
5. *There are some options to help with the cost.*
   - A traditional LTC policy will pay or reimburse for some or all LTC costs. These policies can also become costly over time. And if you don't have one by the time you reach Medicare age, it's unlikely you'll qualify. Insurance companies can consider health conditions when determining eligibility for an LTC policy. In 2019, almost one-third of applicants ages 65–69 were denied coverage.
   - An annuity is essentially a contract with an insurance company. You purchase an annuity that the insurance company pays back over a defined period of time. It's possible to get guaranteed payments for life, even if the amount paid back exceeds the original investment.
   - Combination or hybrid products are life insurance with an LTC rider. These relatively new products combine life insurance with LTC insurance. The idea is that policy benefits will always be paid, in life insurance or LTC. A policyholder can access some or all of the policy's death benefit for LTC that meets the company's requirements.
   - A Health Savings Account pays for qualified medical expenses. According to the IRS, qualified

medical expenses "also include amounts paid for qualified long-term care services and limited amounts paid for any qualified long-term care insurance contract."

- A reverse mortgage is a special type of home equity loan that allows the mortgage holder to receive cash against the value of a home without selling it. That cash could pay for LTC.
- Medicare Advantage plans can cover supplemental health care benefits for "daily maintenance." Some plans offer one benefit; others may offer more. The offerings can have limits, require prior authorization, and impose network limitations. Chances are an individual may need more services than the plan offers. For instance, one plan covers 30 personal aide visits of up to four hours in a calendar year. (See chap. 3, "Making Your Medicare Path Decision.")
- Medicaid is a program funded jointly by individual states and the federal government. One of the benefits is LTC. Every state has its own enrollment process, qualification criteria, and policies. Find information about a specific state program at www.medicare-links.com/apply-for-medicaid.

As you consider how to pay for LTC, consult with the appropriate professionals.

LTC presents many challenges, but everyone needs a plan. It's never too late to put together an LTC plan, your personal strategy for handling decisions in the future.

Here are some steps to help you get started.

- Learn about LTC, the different options, and what's available in your community.
- Work with a trusted financial advisor to develop a plan to cover the costs.

- Determine who can play a role in your plan. Do not expect your family to be the sole source of support.
- Explore community resources and caregiving options.
- Incorporate your wishes into the plan. Do you have an up-to-date will, advance health care directive, and durable POA for health care? Include in your plan important financial information and your LTC wishes.
- Share the plan with family members, health care providers, and anyone whom you believe will be involved or needs to know it.

LTC Insurance and a Designated Individual: Learn from My True-Life Story

My dad, Rusty, had paid for an LTC policy for many years. Then one day, I was waiting for him to get ready for a doctor's appointment, and I decided to check his mail, the first time I had ever done that. I found a cancelation notice for nonpayment of premiums from the LTC insurance company.

"Dad, why are you not paying the premiums for this policy?"

"Because I have Medicare and my pipe trades policy. I don't need that one."

"Dad, get out your checkbook. We're going to the FedEx office and sending in the payment."

Three weeks later, we found Dad semicomatose. He was diagnosed with kidney failure, a complication from prostate cancer, and could not manage his care. He was admitted to an LTC facility where he lived until his death 13 months later. The LTC policy paid its share every day, the difference between my dad keeping or having to sell his farm.

Dad fell for one of the biggest Medicare myths ever: that Medicare covers LTC. He wasn't alone in thinking that. Thankfully, I caught the problem in time and saved his policy.

After things settled down, I dug into why he was so close to cancelation. His cancelation letter said the designated individual did not respond to the cancelation notice.

The application process for an LTC policy includes unintentional lapse protection. This provision can protect those who develop a cognitive impairment and are no longer paying the premiums. The insured can designate at least one individual to receive a notice for nonpayment of the premium. The insurance company will send a notice to that individual when the premium is 30 days overdue. This notice will include specifics, such as when the payment was due initially, the date of cancelation if payment is not received, and how to avoid termination of the policy.

Dad had designated me as that individual and provided my contact information, but I never got any notifications. As my father's POA, I called the company and discovered the insurance agent misspelled my name and street and listed the wrong zip code. There was no way that letter would find its way to my house.

Here are some valuable tips so you can avoid what almost happened to my father.

- Make sure your family members with LTC insurance have a designated individual.
- Verify that the name and contact information are correct. This is also a good tip for anyone who has a policy. After the incident with Dad, I contacted my LTC insurer to confirm information on my policy.
- Take timely action if you are the designated person and get a notice about nonpayment of premium.

Questions and Answers about Other Important Things You Need to Know

Can I enroll in Medicare during the OEP?

If it is your time to enroll during October, November, or December, meaning you are in your Initial Enrollment Period (IEP) or you qualify for a Part B SEP, you can and should enroll so you don't miss your opportunity. But technically, you are not enrolling during the OEP.

However, if you didn't enroll when you should have, you can't do it during the OEP. You must wait until the General Enrollment Period, January 1–March 31.

If my 65th birthday is in November, must I get everything done by December 7?

The OEP applies to those already enrolled in Medicare. If you are not yet enrolled, you have your seven-month IEP to enroll. The December 7 deadline does not apply to you.

Is there a limit on the number of times I can switch Part D drug plans during the OEP?

You can make one change during one OEP. But there is no limit on the number of years you can enroll in a different Part D drug or Medicare Advantage plan during the OEP. Those who take several medications and/or very costly ones likely will get better prices and coverage if they switch frequently. Medicare Advantage networks and benefits can change every year, so a change may be necessary.

Can I get a different Medigap policy during Open Enrollment?

The OEP only applies to Part D drug and Medicare Advantage plans.

You can apply for a new Medigap policy at any time during the year. However, remember, if you don't have a guaranteed issue right, you may be subject to medical underwriting.

When can I drop my Medicare Advantage plan and purchase a Medigap policy?

Even though you can apply for a Medigap policy at any time, there are only two times every year that you can disenroll from your Medicare Advantage plan: the OEP and the Medicare Advantage OEP. And remember, depending on your situation, you may or may not have a guaranteed issue right.

Must I renew Medicare every year?

Once you are enrolled in Part A and Part B, you are set for life. You do not have to renew your enrollment. Every year, you do have the opportunity to evaluate your drug or Medicare Advantage plan. If you decide not to change, the coverage will renew automatically.

Can I change my Medicare and Social Security representatives?

You can add or update your Medicare personal representative at any time through your MyMedicare.gov account. (See chap. 6, "Living with Medicare.") The 1-800-MEDICARE Authorization to Disclose Personal Health Information form notes that you have the right to revoke your authorization at any time; you would send a written request to the address noted on the form.

Contact your Medicare plan representative if you need to update your authorizations.

Once you do an advance designation of a Social Security representative payee, you'll receive a notice from Social Security every year. This will confirm your designation and give you a chance to make changes.

What is an advance directive?

An advance directive is a legal document that expresses your wishes regarding medical treatment if you are unable to make decisions because of an injury or serious illness.

You read in Chapter 1 about a medical POA for health care decisions, one type of advance directive. The person who holds your POA can make medical decisions for you.

A living will is another directive. This document identifies treatments, such as tube feedings, cardiopulmonary resuscitation, or dialysis, that you would or would not want at the end of your life when terminally ill. It informs the person holding your medical POA about your wishes.

Know these important points.

- Advance directives must be in writing.
- It may be best to consult an attorney for help since each state has its own forms and requirements.
- Once executed, give a copy to your doctor and health care agents.
- Keep original documents in a safe but accessible place.
- You can cancel a directive at any time, as long as you are of sound mind.
- Update the directive with any significant change in your medical condition or marital status, and at least every 10 years. Share the updates with those who need to know.

If Medicare covers nursing homes and home care services, how come it doesn't pay for LTC?

Part A does indeed cover inpatient care in a skilled nursing facility (SNF) and home health care, common settings for LTC.

So you may wonder, If a person moves into a nursing home because she needs LTC or a home care agency sends an aide to the home to help a patient with bathing, why doesn't

Medicare pay? The simple answer is that Medicare pays for care that is skilled, meaning that it requires the skills of a registered nurse, physical therapist, occupational therapist, or speech-language pathologist. If the average nonmedical person can provide the care without additional training, the care is not skilled, and Medicare will not pay for it.

The person is in a nursing home because she is not safe at home and needs help with ADL. It doesn't take a nurse to bathe a person. Contrast that to skilled care. The person who had a stroke goes to a nursing home for rehabilitation. Once home, a physical therapist visits to set up a home program and coordinate equipment.

Epilogue

Final Words

Congratulations. You made it to the end of this book, and you're still standing (or sitting). Remember these five important takeaways.

- *Develop a plan.* Even if you're not going to enroll right away, figure out what you need to do about Medicare during your Initial Enrollment Period.
- *Give yourself plenty of time.* Those who wait until the last minute and just want to be done with Medicare take shortcuts, greatly increasing the chances for costly mistakes and coverage problems.
- *Make your own decisions.* You are unique, so you need coverage that will work for you, not what your spouse or friend has.
- *Follow the rules.* Know which doctors to see and pharmacies to use. If a service requires authorization, make sure that's done.
- *Don't put Medicare on autopilot.* Every year, you have the opportunity to review your drug or Medicare Advantage plan. Failing to do that could really cost you. And check www.dianeomdahl.com/updates for current Medicare costs and any other relevant changes.

Now, it's time to apply your book learning and get out into the real world of Medicare.

Appendix: Initial Enrollment Period (IEP) Worksheets

Depending on what day of the month your birthday falls on, use one of these worksheets to identify your IEP. Then, during this time, study your situation and determine what, if anything, you need to do about Medicare.

Your Initial Enrollment Period (IEP)

Use this worksheet if your birthday is the first day of any month.

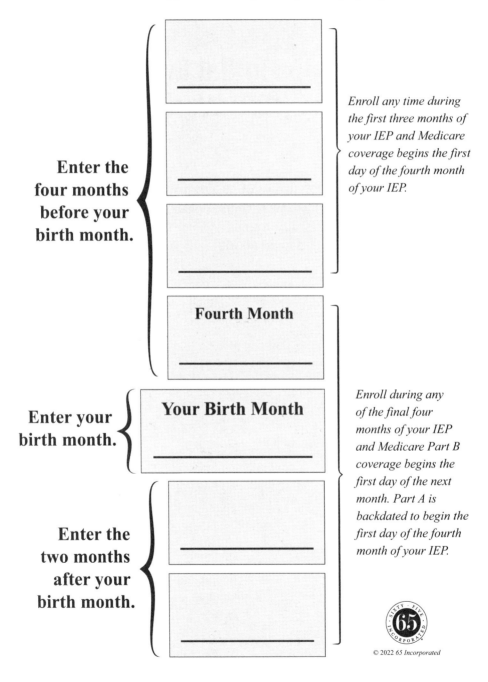

Enter the four months before your birth month.

_____

_____

_____

Enroll any time during the first three months of your IEP and Medicare coverage begins the first day of the fourth month of your IEP.

Fourth Month

_____

Enter your birth month.

Your Birth Month

_____

Enroll during any of the final four months of your IEP and Medicare Part B coverage begins the first day of the next month. Part A is backdated to begin the first day of the fourth month of your IEP.

Enter the two months after your birth month.

_____

_____

Your Initial Enrollment Period (IEP)

Use this worksheet if your birthday is __NOT__ on the first day of any month.

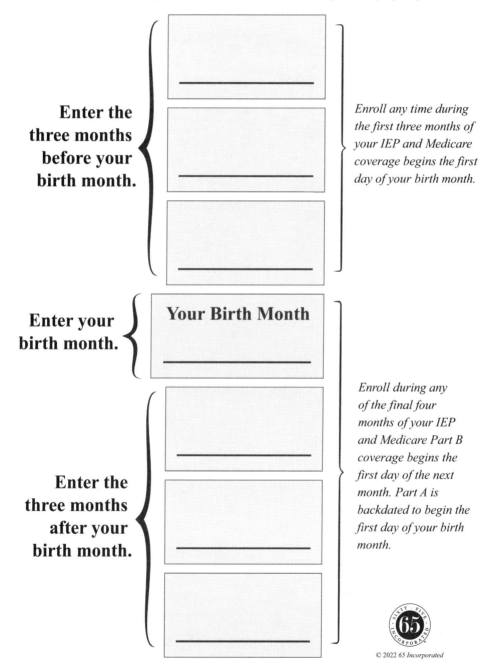

Enter the three months before your birth month.

Enroll any time during the first three months of your IEP and Medicare coverage begins the first day of your birth month.

Your Birth Month

Enter your birth month.

Enroll during any of the final four months of your IEP and Medicare Part B coverage begins the first day of the next month. Part A is backdated to begin the first day of your birth month.

Enter the three months after your birth month.

Acknowledgments

First and foremost, my late husband, Rich Omdahl, was the first one to recognize that not only did Medicare make sense to me, but I could also help others make sense of Medicare.

He had the courage to leave the corporate world and start a business based on my knowledge. Our first product was a guide to Medicare service delivery for home health care agencies—the first of its kind in the industry. After a 23-year run with that business, Rich encouraged me to start over, this time helping consumers with Medicare. He would have approved of a book to help them make smart Medicare decisions.

Don Gawronski, my content and editing guru for more than 30 years. His help on the newsletters and publications we've done together prepared me for this massive project.

Michael Caughill, my book-writing mentor. He helped guide this novice through the process.

Melinda Caughill, my business partner, for stepping up to the plate after Rich died. Rich would have loved working on i65.

Rachelle and Dan Cehanovich, my go-to family for keeping my home, cars, and life in working order and my freezer full of great meals.

Charlie and Jacob, my grandsons, for doing their very best to keep their "old grandma" in working order.

Index

Page numbers followed by *f* and *t* refer to figures and tables, respectively.

About the Author

Nationally known Medicare expert, DIANE J. OMDAHL is a registered nurse with a master's degree in Health Services Administration. For more than 30 years, she has been a true pioneer in the field of Medicare. Diane launched her first business in the basement of her home and grew it into a multi-million dollar company providing Medicare education for home health agencies.

In 2012, Diane cofounded her latest company, *65 Incorporated,* with her daughter Melinda Caughill. *65 Incorporated* provides America's seniors with unbiased, individualized Medicare enrollment guidance through fee-for-service, one-on-one consultations.

Diane is also the brain behind the i65 Medicare Optimization software for financial professionals. i65 empowers these professionals to offer accurate Medicare guidance to their clients without being Medicare experts themselves.

65 Incorporated and i65 are not affiliated with the sale of Medicare insurance products in any way, thus giving clients a peace of mind that the recommendations being made are always in their best interest.

Diane writes about Medicare at Forbes.com and has been featured in numerous publications, including *USA Today, The Washington Post, The Wall Street Journal – MarketWatch,* Kiplinger, CBS MoneyWatch and many others.

You can learn more at 65incorporated.com and i65.com.